Closure and Mahler's Music
The Role of Secondary Parameters

University of Pennsylvania Press
Studies in the Criticism and Theory of Music

Leonard B. Meyer, General Editor

Janet M. Levy. *Beethoven's Compositional Choices: The Two Versions of opus 18, No. 1, First Movement*. 1982

Robert O. Gjerdingen. *A Classic Turn of Phrase: Music and the Psychology of Convention*. 1987

Lee A. Rothfarb. *Ernst Kurth as Theorist and Analyst*. 1989

Leonard B. Meyer. *Style and Music: Theory, History, and Ideology*. 1989

Robert G. Hopkins. *Closure and Mahler's Music: The Role of Secondary Parameters*. 1990

Closure and Mahler's Music

The Role of Secondary Parameters

Robert G. Hopkins

University of Pennsylvania Press
Philadelphia

Library of Congress Cataloging-in-Publication Data

Hopkins, Robert G.
   Closure and Mahler's music : the role of secondary parameters /
Robert G. Hopkins
      p.   cm. — (Studies in the criticism and theory of music)
   Based on the author's thesis (Ph.D., University of Pennsylvania,
1983) under title: Secondary parameters and closure in the
symphonies of Gustav Mahler.
   Includes bibliographical references.
   ISBN 0-8122-8215-9
   1. Closure (Music) 2. Mahler, Gustav, 1860–1911—Criticism and
interpretation. I. Title. II. Series
MT6.H583C6 1990
781.2—dc20   89-21448
                                                       CIP
                                                       MN

For my parents

CONTENTS

PREFACE

This book attempts to demonstrate the importance of secondary parameters in articulating closure. It is not only a study of Mahler's innovative and influential ways of creating closure by using secondary parameters rather than relying on cadential closure, but also an investigation of musical closure in general—how it may be defined, how it may be perceived—and, in particular, how secondary parameters may contribute to it.

After years of concentrating on pitches and pitch structures in music, theorists of Western music are starting to expand their focus to include the examination of other parameters, most notably durations. This book lays the foundation for a theory of secondary parameters that with much further study and refinement will eventually account for our perception of processes and patterns in these parameters.

In considering secondary parameters, all kinds of questions arise about how the various musical parameters interact to generate musical structures, and how listeners discern those structures. Such questions are probably impossible to answer now, because we lack a sufficient understanding of how listeners perceive music. We need to comprehend how we perceive individual parametric processes and patterns, and then we can proceed to the far more complicated matter of how musical parameters interact to create formal structures.

This study suggests ways in which the parameters of music act individually, and interact collectively, to create closure. It is my hope that the suppositions and conclusions here will prompt scholars to test various hypotheses about our perception of closure. This book, then, should lead to further research in the psychology of music. Though closure is a fundamental concept in music theory and analysis, one searches in vain for a thorough treatment of the topic, and for experimental evidence that accounts for our perception of it in music. Much has been written about tonal closure, of course, but little has been done to investigate how all the parameters of music, including dynamics and timbre, act and interact to create closure. This book is a first step.

*　　*　　*

A word about the musical examples: all parts are written at their actual sounding pitch, and where practical the orchestration is indicated. Where a single stave contains a conflation of various individual parts, no instruments are designated. When referring to a particular pitch in the text, I will use the pitch notation suggested by the Acoustical Society of America: middle C is C4 (the D above is D4); higher octave Cs are C5, C6, and so on; lower Cs are C3, C2, and so on.

This book is based on my Ph.D. dissertation "Secondary Parameters and Closure in the Symphonies of Gustav Mahler" (University of Pennsylvania, 1983), and has been greatly influenced by the work of Wallace Berry, Leonard B. Meyer, Eugene Narmour, and Barbara Herrnstein Smith. In particular, the debts owed to Leonard B. Meyer are especially numerous and apparent. My heartfelt thanks go to Professor Meyer for the invaluable help I received in writing this study. I am also especially indebted to Eugene Narmour for his many helpful suggestions, and to my wife Kris for her loving support. Finally, I am grateful to Hamilton College for providing a faculty fellowship during the spring of 1988 when the book was completed.

*   *   *

Permission to reprint excerpts and musical examples in the text is acknowledged from the following sources:

From Bartók, *Music for Strings, Percussion and Celesta.* Copyright 1937 by Universal Editions; copyright renewed 1964. All rights reserved. Copyright and renewal assigned to Boosey & Hawkes, Inc., for the U.S.A. Reprinted by permission. Used by permission of European American Music Distributors Corporation, sole U.S.A. and Canadian agent for Universal Edition, for the territory of the world excluding the U.S.A.

From Bartók, *Concerto for Orchestra.* Copyright 1946 by Hawkes & Son (London) Ltd.; copyright renewed 1973. Reprinted by permission of Boosey & Hawkes, Inc.

From Carter, Etude No. 7 from *Eight Etudes and a Fantasy for Woodwind Quartet.* Copyright 1955 (renewed) by Associated Music Publishers, Inc. International copyright secured. All rights reserved. Reprinted by permission.

From Eliot, "The Hollow Men" from *Collected Poems 1909–1962.* Copyright 1936 by Harcourt Brace Jovanovich, Inc. and copyright 1964, 1963 by T. S. Eliot; reprinted by permission of the publisher.

From Hindemith, Piano Sonata No. 2. Copyright 1936 by B. Schott's Soehne, Mainz; copyright renewed. All rights reserved. Used by permission of European American Music Distributors Corporation, sole U.S.A. and Canadian agent for B. Schott's Soehne.

From Ives, Second Sonata for Violin and Piano. Copyright 1951 by G. Schirmer, Inc.; copyright renewed. International copyright secured. All rights reserved. Reprinted by permission.

CHAPTER 1

Introduction

There is general agreement that tonality as an organizing force weakened during the last part of the nineteenth century and the early part of the twentieth. If so, how were musical processes generated and musical structures articulated in the face of a gradual breakdown of traditional tonal functions? How did composers compensate for the weakening of tonal syntax?

One answer is that secondary parameters such as dynamics and duration became more and more important in shaping musical processes and articulating musical form.[1] If that is true, it is likely that the use of such parameters was not only an effect of the attenuation of tonality, but also a cause. As composers became more reliant on what may be called secondary parameters—those other than tonal melody, tonal harmony, and rhythm—and came to avoid traditional cadences, which had been primarily responsible for establishing and confirming the tonic, tonal syntax would have been further weakened.[2] Thus, the phenomena would be interrelated and interdependent. If that hypothesis is correct, the decline of tonal syntax in the music of the late nineteenth and early twentieth centuries should be matched by a concomitant increase in the importance of secondary parameters.

The works of Gustav Mahler are ideal for testing the hypothesis. In particular the symphonies, which were composed between the years 1885 and 1911, exemplify the gradual breakdown of tonal syntax during that period. Moreover, since Mahler is widely regarded as a transitional composer who had a significant impact on music in the twentieth century, a knowledge of how he compensated for the weakening of tonal syntax should help us better to understand stylistic changes during the first two decades of this century. It may also increase our appreciation of how it is that, despite many passages in later works that are difficult to relate to a tonal center, Mahler's music continues to be very popular with a public that tends to show little affection for most twentieth-century classical music.

This study examines the use and importance of secondary parameters for creating closure in the works of Mahler. Although closure is probably the most important means of articulating music, and it has been frequently discussed by theorists and analysts, previous studies have not addressed the topic of musical closure in any great detail. Yet many analytical and theoretical discussions rest on fundamental assumptions about closure, especially—indeed, almost entirely—tonal closure. One speaks of phrases and periods, ABA forms and sonata forms, only because such formal structures have a sufficient degree of closure. The interaction of all musical parameters creates closure, which of course varies in strength. Consequent phrases are generally more closed than antecedent phrases, for example. The antecedent-consequent period that constitutes the A part of a rounded binary (‖:A:‖:B A:‖) is more closed when it occurs after the B section. The same antecedent-consequent period is yet more closed when it is repeated again to end a minuet and trio movement. As the hierarchy of closure is produced, the form is created.

Determining how musical parameters create a hierarchy of closure is a difficult task. This book begins to address the problem by defining how each individual parameter contributes to closure (and, on the other hand, to mobility), and discussing how one might integrate the various closural and nonclosural aspects of the many parameters in order to determine hierarchic levels. Such work is vitally important, as Eugene Narmour has observed:

> In a true hierarchical analysis . . . closure cannot be treated as a byproduct of the existence of prior transforms but rather must be regarded as the central issue governing the very emergence of levels since degree of closure is the crucial factor by which hierarchical levels come into being or are denied existence. Thus, if what is desired is a truly hierarchical conception of analysis, we must come to grips with this matter of closure and nonclosure.[3]

What is considered closed or not closed is determined, ultimately, by the listener. Closure is a psychological phenomenon that depends upon the listener's perception of the patterns and processes in the music. Unfortunately, psychological perception in music, while the focus of ongoing research by a growing number of scholars, is not well understood. In general, studies of musical perception are necessarily restricted to the examination of processes or patterns in a very few parameters—often one or two. Researchers are just now laying the foundation for future study of the ways in which the complex interactions of all musical parameters influence musical perception. This study should suggest fruitful approaches for experimental research on how the individual parameters of music contribute to closure (and mobility), as well as how musical parameters interact to produce closure.

And it is the effect of *all* the parameters that is crucially important. One problem in studying closure is that the theory and analysis of Western tonal music have directed attention almost exclusively to melody, harmony, and, to a lesser extent, rhythm—the primary parameters of tonal music. The secondary parameters have been virtually ignored, though they play a significant role in emphasizing and creating closure. When theorists speak of closure in tonal music, they generally mean cadential closure, where a cadence is defined as "a melodic or harmonic configuration that creates a sense of repose or resolution."[4] Cadences are classified according to their harmonic progression and voice leading, not with respect to durational patterns, register, timbre, or dynamics. But even in tonal music not all closure is cadential closure, and the interaction of the various musical parameters, not just melody and harmony, defines closural strength.

One aim of this book, then, is to analyze closure in terms of all musical parameters, and to examine specifically how the various secondary parameters contribute to closure. Chapter 2 begins by defining closure and discussing the nature of closure in Western music, including how it was usually produced by the primary parameters of tonal pitch and harmony in music of the late eighteenth and nineteenth centuries before the role of tonality as an organizing force was greatly diminished. Once we understand that, we can judge how and to what extent Mahler's means of creating closure were different from his predecessors'. Of course, the chapter is not intended to provide a comprehensive study of closure in tonal music of the late eighteenth and nineteenth centuries; rather, my aim is to discuss only the most salient points, enough to provide a basis for comparison with closure in Mahler's works.

Chapter 3 deals with secondary parameters and how they can be used to create as well as enhance closure. It begins to build a theory of secondary parameters by providing definitions and examples of the parameters and their preferred closural states, and by discussing how secondary parameters act correspondingly to create closure without cadential closure. Since there is general agreement that "Cadences are the principal means by which tonal music projects the sense of one pitch as a central or tonic pitch in a passage or work,"[5] such noncadential closure—what may be called *abating* closure—contributes to the breakdown of traditional tonality while opening up new, creative possibilities for articulating musical form in tonal and nontonal music.

The specific use of secondary parameters to establish closure in the works of Mahler is discussed in the fourth chapter. The focus is on specific examples chosen to illustrate both the imaginative variety of ways in which secondary parameters are used to articulate musical form and the importance of secondary parameters compared to primary parameters for defining musical form. In the same chapter I discuss the basic strategies Mahler employs to establish closure and articulate form.

Finally, I draw conclusions about Mahler's methods of creating closure, identify trends in his use of secondary parametric processes as a means of articulating form, and assess the relative importance of secondary parameters for producing closure in his works, which demonstrate that the attenuation of tonal syntax is generally matched by a concomitant increase in the importance of secondary parameters.

CHAPTER 2

Closure

Closure in music is the sense of satisfactory conclusion that comes with the antici- pated arrival at a state of comparative repose following tension or activity.[1] For closure to occur, it is necessary—but not sufficient—for a discernible process or pattern in one or more musical parameters to imply a particular point of conclusion. When the process or pattern is relatively complete and stable, we say it is closed, and if its effect is not outweighed by ongoing processes in some other parameter(s), the listener will perceive closure.[2] Thus, closure is a psychological phenomenon that depends upon the listener's perception of the organization of musical elements,[3] and hence the listener's understanding of the action and interaction of all the parameters of music. In this study, closure is viewed as just one of several ways of defining separable musical events, and is reserved for those instances in which an arrival at a point of comparative repose has been implied by the organization of the music, as determined by all the parameters.

Not all endings are closed. If the listener cannot discern a process or pattern, the music will seem to *stop*—to terminate—rather than to *close*.[4] Typically we become aware that such a passage is over when another passage, whether new or familiar, begins. If the stop occurs at the end of a work, the silence following the last sound (and, no doubt, visual cues such as the performers putting down their instruments) tells us that the piece has ended.

Closing, therefore, should be differentiated from stopping.[5] Randomly gener- ated tones, antiphonal choirs, and ostinatos stop; a perfect authentic cadence closes. Barbara Smith expresses it well:

> We tend to speak of conclusions when a sequence of events has a relatively high degree of structure, when, in other words, we can perceive these events as related to one another by some principle of organization or design that implies the existence of a definite termination point. Under these circumstances, the occurrence of the terminal event is a confirmation

of expectations that have been established by the structure of the sequence and is usually distinctly gratifying. The sense of stable conclusiveness, finality, or "clinch" which we experience at that point is what is referred to here as *closure*.[6]

Closure is a very complex phenomenon, primarily because the parameters of music act and interact in diverse ways. In a specific passage, some parametric processes may support closure, others may promote mobility, and still others may be neutral. Moreover, not all parameters are equally important. In any particular style of music some parameters are more important than others for creating closure. In music of the classical period, for example, harmony is more important than dynamics.

One approach to studying closure is to consider how processes in each musical parameter can affect our perception of closure. Change in a parameter will produce a sense of motion—passage from one state to another—while the absence of change will produce a sense of motionlessness.[7] Only a sense of motion can lead to closure, since closure is the *arrival* at a state of relative rest—not merely the condition of rest. Closure should not be confused with the repose that can be produced by the absence of motion or by undirected motion.

Undirected motion, generated by changes in a parameter that are alternating or unpredictable, does not lead to closure because there is no discernible process or design that can imply a point of conclusion. Undirected motion can stop, but it cannot close. This can lead to frustration on the part of listeners who cannot discern directed motion in the parameters of pitch and harmony in nontonal music. When they find pitch processes unpredictable, listeners are forced to rely on processes in other parameters (such as dynamics and timbre) to establish points of closure.

Often, though, motion created by changes in a parameter is directed motion, which can lead to closure. Directed motion is either *intensifying* or *abating*.[8] Intensifying motion generally promotes mobility, and abating motion typically promotes closure. Intensifying changes tend either to heighten tension, as constantly increasing dynamics often do, or to increase activity, as ever shorter durations tend to do. On the other hand, abating changes tend either to lower tension, as constantly decreasing dynamics typically do, or to lessen activity, as ever augmenting durations tend to do. In general, then, a crescendo or accelerando (provided that notated durations are not increasing in length) is intensifying, whereas a decrescendo or ritardando (providing that notated durations are not diminishing) is abating.

An intensifying series of elements is an *intensification*. It builds to a *climax*, the point of greatest tension or activity in a series of elements. An abating series of elements is an *abatement*. It leads to a *depression*, the point of least tension or activity in a series of elements. In Example 2.1, a dynamic climax occurs on the first beat of measure 3, and a dynamic depression occurs at the end of measure 5.

The intensifying crescendo in measures 1–3 of Example 2.1 is followed by an abating diminuendo in measures 4–5. Although pitch is constant throughout, and thus neutral with respect to closure, the rise and fall in dynamic level establishes a clear

EXAMPLE 2.1. Carter, Etude No. 7 from *Eight Etudes and a Fantasy for Woodwind Quartet,* mm. 1–6. Copyright 1955 (renewed) by Associated Music Publishers, Inc. International copyright secured. All rights reserved. Reprinted by permission.

pattern that suggests closure may come with the return to the opening dynamic level. The return to the opening timbre at the end of measure 5 supports closure, as does the relatively long time interval between attack points in the last half of measure 5 and the first part of measure 6. (The overall pattern of attack points in measures 4–6 is ♩ ♩ ♩ ♩ ♩ ♩ ♩.) Closure is thus achieved when the piano dynamic in the clarinet returns at the end of measure 5.

Like the dynamic intensification in Example 2.1, many intensifications and abatements are characterized by continuous change in a particular parameter. More often, though, changes occur in steps, such as when a motive is immediately repeated at mezzo-forte, then forte, then fortissimo dynamic levels. Stepped changes are also commonly found in the parameters of pitch, harmony, and duration.

EXAMPLE 2.2. Chopin, Scherzo in E Major, op. 54, mm. 585–93.

Most often, changes in a parameter (whether continuous or stepped changes) are not consistently abating or intensifying, but rather reveal an overall abating or intensifying trend. Measures 4–5 of Example 2.1, for instance, lack a continuous decrescendo, but one easily perceives a generally decreasing dynamic level. In the same way, the right-hand part of Example 2.2 is generally descending in pitch, thereby creating an abating pattern. Throughout this book we will be concerned primarily with abating and intensifying trends in various parameters.

In any given passage, different parameters can have different functions. If they do, the parameters are *noncongruent*.[9] In such cases we may describe the passage as intensifying with respect to certain parameters, but abating or static with respect to others. Consider Example 2.2, in which the accelerando is intensifying while the decrescendo and the generally descending pitch pattern in the right hand are abating. In this example, then, duration is noncongruent with dynamics and registral pitch.[10]

Even when parameters have the same function—are *congruent*—the succession of changes in each can begin and end at different times. If the processes begin at the same time, they are *initially synchronized;* if they end together, they are *terminally synchronized.* In Example 2.2, the decrescendo and the descending pitch pattern are initially synchronized in measure 585, but they are not terminally synchronized since the pitch pattern stabilizes in measure 593 while the decrescendo continues.

Highly synchronized parameters are those in which the successions of changes begin and end together. When parameters are both congruent and highly synchronized, they are *corresponding.* In Example 2.3, the chromatically ascending pitches

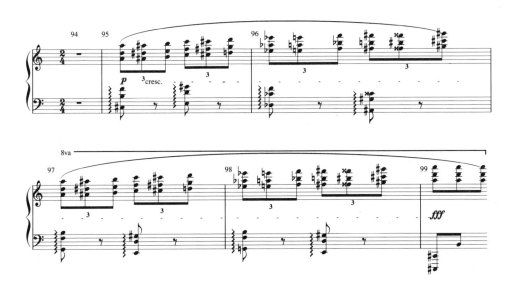

EXAMPLE 2.3. Scriabin, Etude, op. 65, no. 3, mm. 94–99.

in the right hand are accompanied by a crescendo which begins and ends with the chromatic ascent; registral pitch and dynamics are corresponding. The intensifying changes in the two parameters build to a strong climax at the beginning of measure 99. The more processes are synchronized, the clearer the structural goal.

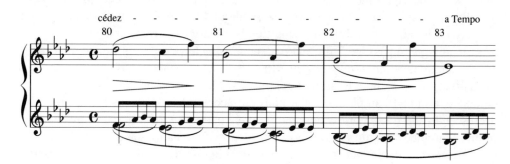

EXAMPLE 2.4. Debussy, *Suite bergamasque,* no. 4 (*Passepied*), mm. 80–83.

In Example 2.4, abating changes in registral pitch (the descending, conjunct lines D♭ to E♭ in the top staff and F to G in the bottom staff) are matched by abating changes in durational patterning (gradually longer durations owing to the *cédez* indication) and dynamics. Thus, registral pitch, durations, and dynamics are all corresponding. The greater the number of corresponding parameters, the stronger the process.

The terms intensification and abatement are especially useful in discussing secondary parameters such as dynamics.[11] We can apply them to the primary parameters of tonal music as well, but only in a more general sense. With respect to harmony, for example, chords with dominant function are on the whole most tensive and chords with tonic function most stable, but chords with other functions are less clearly defined. A chord progression that leads away from the tonic or moves to the dominant may in general be hypothesized as an intensification; one that leads away from the dominant or moves to the tonic may be thought of as an abatement. Typically, as in an authentic cadence, an abatement is produced by the direct resolution of the dominant chord to the tonic. With respect to the parameter of tonal pitch, leading tones are usually most tensive and tones that function as tonics are usually most stable. In general, then, a series of pitches that leads away from the tonic or moves to the leading tone could be considered an intensification; a series that moves away from the leading tone or leads to the tonic would be an abatement.

Closure is the result of directed motion toward repose following tension or activity. Two basic processes establish closure: one that leads from a point of tension more or less gradually to a point of repose—that is, an abatement—and one that builds in tension until reaching a point of reversal, whereupon stability and rest are achieved—that is, an intensification that builds to a climax and then quickly (perhaps immediately) reaches repose. The first process is typically one in which secondary parameters create abating closure, whereas the second process is ordinarily one in which primary parameters create cadential closure. Which of these ways composers choose to create closure affects our perception of the character of the closure. Abating closure tends to be more passive, calm, or peaceful, whereas cadential closure that features a great intensification prior to the resolution to the tonic is perceived as more forceful, emphatic, vigorous. In any case closure itself, as differentiated from the process leading to it, is a state of comparative repose following tension or activity. Thus, closure is characterized by a relative absence of stress.

Different kinds of delaying tactics can be used to manipulate the implied point of closure. Delays generally contribute to a local rise in tension that makes an expected resolution more satisfying.[12] Accordingly, delays are most effective toward the end of a pattern, and especially at the end of a movement or work, when closure seems imminent. In tonal music, for instance, typical harmonic progressions leading to the dominant seventh, such as $\mathrm{ii}_6\text{--}\mathrm{I}_4^6\text{--}\mathrm{V}_7$, imply that closure will arrive with the tonic that resolves the dominant seventh. Occasionally a delay is caused by the interruption of

EXAMPLE 2.5. Beethoven, Symphony No. 3 in E♭ Major, op. 55 ("Eroica"), I, mm. 667–73.

the cadential process, as in the case of a cadenza in a solo concerto. Sometimes a delay is created by a deceptive alteration in a process directed toward closure, such as the use of a deceptive cadence. Other times a delay is produced by an abrupt, typically unexpected change in one or more secondary parameters. That is illustrated in the passage given in Example 2.5. The perfect authentic cadence in measures 670–73 creates strong closure with respect to melody and harmony, but our overall sense of closure—of satisfactory conclusion—is considerably lessened by the suddenly soft dynamic level. The noncongruence between the secondary parameter of dynamics and the primary parameters of melody and harmony forces a delay in final closure until measures 689–91 (not shown in the example), where a fortissimo tonic chord resolves the fortissimo dominant seventh.

Closure varies in strength, depending in part on the number of parameters that create it: the more abating parametric processes, and the fewer intensifying processes, the stronger the closure. The strength of closure also depends upon the importance of the parameters that produce it. The relative importance of a particular parameter varies according to the style of the period, as well as to the style of the composer and the style of the particular work, so what counts as strong closure will often vary from style to style, composer to composer, and work to work. In tonal music the primary parameters of tonal pitch and harmony are more important than other parameters for producing closure. However, abating secondary parameters often provide strong reinforcement of tonal closure at the ends of major sections and the conclusion of the work. At other times secondary parameters can weaken cadential closure by creating instability and mobility through intensification, or (as in Example 2.5) by articulating the beginning of a passage through an abrupt change at the point of primary parametric closure.[13]

Because our perception of closure depends upon our understanding of the processes or patterns in a work, what we consider complete and stable is often conditioned by style.[14] For example, a phrygian cadence is an acceptable final conclusion for Dufay's *Je me complains piteusement,* but not for a work by Handel. A perfect authentic cadence in the dominant at the end of a sonata form exposition in a movement by Mozart would not be considered as complete and stable as the identical cadence transposed to the tonic at the end of the recapitulation. Thus, our perception of closure is often dependent upon our knowledge of stylistic conventions.

A given style may have a number of conventional closing gestures which have been established through repeated use. Typically, conventional (learned) closing gestures are defined by the parameters most important for articulating form and generating musical processes in the style—the *primary* parameters. In tonal music, for instance, the perfect authentic cadence is defined basically by the primary parameters of tonal melody and tonal harmony. Processes and patterns in less important, secondary parameters can also create closure, but such closure does not usually become conventional; at least, it did not until the latter part of the nineteenth century.

There are many other factors, however, that influence our perception of closural strength. For example, other types of musical articulation—a pause, a repetition, the return of something familiar, and the beginning of something new—can strengthen our impression of closure if they follow the arrival at a point of relative rest, since they separate what follows from what has just concluded. That is, closure is strengthened to the extent that what follows is not perceived as a continuation. In a vocal work, the articulations in the text and, if there are instruments, the interaction of the vocal and instrumental parts generally have a great influence on our perception of closure.

Moreover, the strength of closure is partly a consequence of the length of time that repose, once achieved, is sustained. In general, closure is stronger when it is prolonged. For instance, composers of the classical period commonly strengthened primary parametric closure at the ends of large sections and movements by extending the chord of resolution. The extension might be produced by repeating scalar or triadic pitch patterns based on the tonic, reiterating the tonic one or more times, or simply prolonging the tonic chord in some manner. Typically, the longest such extension is saved for the final conclusion, as in the finale of Mozart's Symphony No. 35 in D Major, K. 504. In many tonal works the final chord is marked with a fermata or is otherwise notated as the longest in the piece. When a work ends with the repeat of a previous section, performers and conductors often hold the final chord of the piece beyond its notated duration in order to emphasize final closure.

Since the strength of closure is partly dependent on its length, it follows that no piece of music is absolutely closed. The sense of closure can be decisive and powerful, but it cannot be absolute. Even if all the parameters acted congruently in establishing closure, one could (theoretically, at least) still extend the final chord or note further.

To summarize: closure is relative—it is more or less strong or weak. The strength of closure is determined by the number and the importance of the synchronized parameters that produce it, the nature of the following music, and the length of time that the state of rest is sustained. In addition, our listening perspective affects our perception of closural strength.

As we listen to music, the various points of closure (having varying strengths) create a hierarchy of formal structures. What is considered closed on one level may not be closed on another—that is, it may be heard as part of an ongoing, higher-level organization. A perfect authentic cadence at the end of a consequent phrase in an antecedent-consequent structure will create strong closure on one hierarchic level, but the listener may come to perceive the antecedent-consequent structure as part of a higher-level organization (such as a rounded binary) that has stronger closure. Indeed, we tend to attribute greater strength to closure of higher-level structures even when the concluding passage is essentially identical to the conclusion of a lower-level constituent. Thus, closural strength is understood both prospectively and retrospectively. Or to put it another way, any formal constituent in a musical hierarchy is both open and closed at the same time; the form will be closed on one level when sufficient closure is achieved, but open on a higher level. In music that exhibits hierarchic structure, closure at the end of a phrase is strengthened if the phrase completes one or more higher-level processes or patterns in addition to completing the process or pattern that articulates the phrase.

The perspective of the individual listener is all important. An experienced listener recognizes that the half cadence that ends an antecedent phrase in a Beethoven scherzo produces closure with respect to the phrase (that is, on the level of a phrase), but *at the same time* the antecedent phrase is not closed with respect to the next higher hierarchic level (that is, the period). A consequent phrase brings closure to the period, but the period is open with respect to the rounded binary we expect to hear. When the same consequent phrase (or a varied one) returns following contrasting material, the cadence that ends the phrase also closes the rounded binary. But the rounded binary is open on the next hierarchic level, and we expect the movement to continue with a trio. The repetition of the scherzo after the trio closes the movement, though here again the movement is open with respect to the entire work: we expect a finale to follow.

It should be clear that the listener's experience with style structures informs his or her experience of closure. If a listener is unfamiliar with the style of a work, and cannot anticipate points of closure with much confidence or appreciate how a particular passage fits into a hierarchic structure very easily, then the listener may not be able to perceive a hierarchic structure in the work and may find it "difficult to follow" or "hard to understand." When composers at the beginning of the twentieth century began to write pieces that avoided traditional cadences and conventional tonality altogether, many listeners had trouble discerning closure, no doubt in large part because for them the most important indications of closure—traditional tonal cadences—were missing.[15]

Not only is the listener's ability to perceive relationships crucial to our understanding of closure as defined here, but also the listener must have time—if only an instant—to perceive a relationship that establishes the expectation of a conclusion. One would not ascribe closure to a small-scale event when the listener is not afforded such an opportunity. For example, the return of the note C in a series of eighth-note pitches C-D-C completes a small-scale pattern, but with respect to the overall musical context the return to C does not create closure in and of itself. It is unlikely that the listener will gain a "sense of satisfactory conclusion" with the return to C.[16] If, on the other hand, the pitches were supported by I–V_7–I harmonies, and the durations were sufficiently long, the series could reach closure with the anticipated return of the C and the tonic. Closure depends upon the listener's evaluation of the entire musical context.

It is useful, therefore, to differentiate between closure in an overall musical context, on the one hand, and closure as it relates to a specific parametric process, on the other hand. Writers have used closure in these two different ways when discussing music. Thus one may speak of durational closure, for instance, when a durational process or pattern reaches closure. Since duration is only one of several parameters, however, the durational closure may not be sufficiently strong to create closure with respect to the overall musical context. In such cases we may say that the durational closure creates a *degree* of closure. Then, if one accepts the view that at any point in time music is more or less closed (and more or less open), one can hypothesize that some degree of closure, however slight, articulates musical events on all hierarchic levels. Still, a listener makes judgments about closure based on *all* parametric processes and patterns, so closure does not occur whenever there is a degree of repose (as defined by one musical parameter, for example), but rather whenever there is a satisfactory conclusion (defined by the overall musical context). At some point a perceptual threshold is crossed and the listener determines that a passage is closed—that it is complete and stable and unlikely to be continued.[17]

An important aspect of closure is that it prepares the listener for something else: it creates in the listener the expectation that there will be something new, a return of familiar material, a variation, or a repetition. Final—that is, last—closure creates the expectation of silence, the expectation that there will be no continuation, as Barbara Smith has observed:

> It reinforces the feeling of finality, completion, and composure which we value in all works of art; and it gives ultimate unity and coherence to the reader's [listener's] experience of the poem [work] by providing a point from which all the preceding elements may be viewed comprehensively and their relations grasped as part of a significant design.[18]

At times closure occurs without confirmation of the listener's expectations. A surprise ending can thwart expectations of resolution and require the listener to re-evaluate retrospectively the implications of the processes and patterns in the music. To quote Barbara Smith again:

> The surprise ending is one which forces and rewards a readjustment of the reader's expectations; it justifies itself retrospectively. A disappointing ending, on the other hand, is not accommodated by such a readjustment; it remains unjustified and the reader's expectations remain foiled. . . . Whereas a surprise ending provides a perspective point from which the reader can now appreciate a significant pattern, principle, or motive not grasped before, a disappointing conclusion reveals nothing about the poem's structure.[19]

The first movement of Beethoven's Eighth Symphony is a good example of a movement with a surprise ending. The listener anticipates final closure after the authentic cadences in measures 354–55, 358–60, 362–65, and the reiterated tonic chords and diminuendo in measures 366 and following. The surprise is the fact that final (that is, last) closure comes with the repetition of a thematic motive which had previously been used as an *opening* gesture. The motive is marked with a bracket in Example 2.6a, which gives the primary theme of the movement as stated in the recapitulation. In measures 372–73 (Example 2.6b) the strings play the motive as a *closing* gesture.

The surprise ending forces the listener to re-evaluate his or her expectations. The listener realizes retrospectively that the motive always had the potential to be a

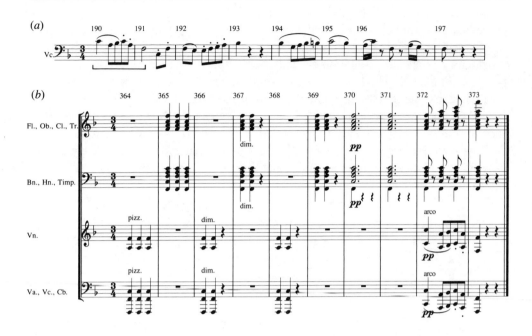

EXAMPLE 2.6. Beethoven, Symphony No. 8 in F Major, op. 93, I: (*a*) mm. 190–97; (*b*) mm. 364–73.

closing gesture, but the potential was not realized until the conclusion of the movement.

Except for endings that require and reward a reconsideration of the listener's expectations, closure is not usually experienced retrospectively.[20] It is generally anticipated, though perhaps only momentarily, and subsequently realized at a point implied by unfolding designs and processes in the music. Closure is thus differentiated not only from stopping, but also from other means of articulation such as a pause, the return of familiar material, or the beginning of essentially different material, all of which can indicate in retrospect the end of a musical passage. It seems useful to distinguish such endings—or terminations—from true conclusions, which are defined by closure.

*   *   *

In order to consider closure in more detail, we must examine the ways in which musical elements can be related to one another: (1) by conformance, (2) in a syntactic process, or (3) in a process defined by one or more secondary parameters. All three kinds of relationships can help to produce closure by implying a specific point of conclusion. In the rest of this book we will examine closure as it relates to these three areas—in particular the third area, which is discussed in detail in chapters 3 and 4. The remainder of this chapter will be devoted to discussion of conformant relationships and syntactic processes.

CONFORMANT RELATIONSHIPS

Musical events that are similar to one another are conformant.[21] Conformance may be relatively strong or weak, depending upon whether the events are more or less similar. Of course, our ability to recognize conformant relationships depends not only on how similar the two events are, but also on how memorable the model is and how much time separates the events. In general, the more two events are separated in time, the more striking the model must be and the more similar the events must be if one is to perceive a conformant relationship.

Closure can be enhanced—that is, strengthened—or created by the return of an event that conforms to a previous event. If A and A′ represent conformant events, then the statement of A′ following both A and some contrasting event B would constitute a return.[22] Closure would be strengthened for several reasons. First, A′ presents familiar music. Based on prior experience, then, the listener anticipates how the music will continue. Accordingly, A′ implies the existence of a specific ending point: the same point that closed A.[23] The return of familiar music after a contrasting section also produces an impression of symmetry and unity that contributes to the sense of closure. These properties of regularity, symmetry, and simplicity belong to what Gestalt psychologists call a "good" pattern.[24]

It is important to realize that closure can be enhanced, but not created, through the principle of return. Closure at the end of A′ still depends upon abating changes in one or more parameters.[25] Indeed, most of the time our recognition of A and A′ as musical events depends upon closure at the end of each, though an event can instead be articulated by silence, the repetition of something familiar, or an abrupt and clear change in one or more parameters.

Another point needs to be considered here. Once a series of elements has been established as an event, the return of only part of it will be considered incomplete. If, however, in the course of the work the fragment comes to represent the entire original event, then an occurrence of the fragment may represent a return and closure is reinforced.

Of course, conformant relationships do not always support closure. For example, the immediate repetition of the same or a similar event will not create a sense of return, but instead often creates a desire for change, continuation, and closure. Rather than a balanced structure involving a return after some contrasting event, the constant reiteration creates an open, additive structure. Each statement of the event may be closed, but no higher-level organization implies a specific conclusion. The theme and variations form exemplifies this kind of structure, where each variation is an event. Often a composer will use some secondary parameter(s), such as dynamics or duration, to give shape to the variations, or will bring back the original statement of the theme (thus, a return). If there is no clear differentiation of parts, closure is dependent on extramusical means, such as textual closure at the end of a strophic song or abating changes introduced by the performer(s).

The preceding discussion is subject to an important qualification. Our awareness of the reason for the repetition of a figure will affect our understanding. If we have determined that a figure is an ostinato, for example, we do not expect change in the figure. Nor do reiterated V_7–I cadences imply change, since we understand them collectively as a closing gesture emphasizing stability and repose.[26] The repeated cadences create stasis and, frequently, the expectation of silence. Even so, because a series of cadences creates an additive structure, final closure is weakened unless some other process or design implies a specific point of termination.[27]

So far we have discussed only *intra*-opus conformant relationships. Closure can be emphasized because of *inter*-opus conformant relationships as well. When a particular closing gesture is repeated in several different works, it becomes part of the style of the composer(s) who uses it. As listeners become familiar with a given style, they learn to associate such conventional gestures with closure. Of course, it is likely that the gestures are effective in establishing or strengthening closure to begin with; otherwise they probably would not have been copied. Their effectiveness in a particular work is enhanced, though, because they conform to gestures that close phrases, sections, or movements in other works familiar to the listener. Experienced listeners recognize such gestures as an indication that the phrase, section, or movement is at an end, and they can anticipate a specific point of conclusion based upon their experience.

EXAMPLE 2.7. Mozart: (*a*) Symphony No. 40 in G Minor, K. 550, IV, mm. 271–77; (*b*) String Quartet No. 4 in C Major, K. 157, I, mm. 39–42; (*c*) Piano Concerto No. 23 in A Major, K. 488, I, mm. 60–62.

Since the listener's experience of a specific conventional closing gesture is often distant in time from the experience of closing gestures that conform to it, the strength of the conformant relationship rests on the simplicity and clear likeness of the gestures being compared.[28] The stronger the conformant relationship, the stronger is the sense of closure.

Example 2.7 presents three instances of one conventional closing gesture that was part of the style of Mozart. The gesture combines forceful closure in both primary parameters of tonal pitch and harmony, and closure is enhanced by inter-opus conformance. The basic pitch motion is a stepwise descent from the fifth degree of the scale to the tonic. The abating motion 5–4–3–2 implies the tonic as its goal, but the tonic is reached only after a brief reversal in direction. The reversal (measures 275, 41, and 61 in Example 2.7a, 2.7b, and 2.7c, respectively) exemplifies a local heightening of tension, which is most effective when the listener anticipates the imminent termination of a process or pattern. The tonic is emphasized by the further descent to the leading tone (which implies a resolution to the tonic) and return to the tonic. With respect to tonal pitch, then, this closing gesture is quite convincing.[29] The harmonic closure created by the progression ii^6_5–I^6_4–$\text{V}_{(7)}$–I may be even more compelling. The first three chords of the progression build intensity and strongly imply a resolution to the tonic. The implication is especially forceful in Example 2.7c because a seventh is added (in an inner voice) to the dominant chord in measure 61. In all three instances the durational pattern in the bass supports the harmonic process: the driving quarter notes of Example 2.7a and eighth notes of 2.7b and 2.7c are followed by a longer tonic note which marks a reduction in activity. The beats of rest that follow the tonic in Examples 2.7a and 2.7c emphasize closure. Thus, the parameters of tonal pitch, harmony, and to a lesser extent duration combine to make the conventional gesture illustrated in Example 2.7 a potent force for creating closure.

Example 2.8, on the other hand, presents a conventional closing gesture that is not inherently strong, though closure is strengthened by inter-opus conformance. The gesture consists of three tonic chords of equal duration which usually follow a rest. It is typically employed at the end of a movement or work, and that is the case in the three instances shown in Example 2.8. Unlike the closing gesture of Example 2.7, however, this gesture by itself does not create strong closure; it mostly reinforces stability and repose by reiterating the tonic.[30] In each of the excerpts given in Example 2.8 strong closure had already been created by a perfect authentic cadence and prolongation of the tonic chord shortly before the excerpt begins.[31] In the last movement of the Haydn symphony, a perfect authentic cadence occurs in measures 202–3 and the tonic is prolonged by a series of repeated perfect authentic cadences. In the opening movement of Beethoven's First Symphony, a perfect authentic cadence at measures 276–77 is followed by a prolongation of the tonic. In Example 2.8c a perfect authentic cadence occurs in measures 475–77. In each of these movements the final three tonic chords signal that it is at an end;[32] they inform listeners that the

EXAMPLE 2.8. (*a*) Haydn, Symphony No. 85 in B♭ Major, IV, mm. 212–20; (*b*) Beethoven, Symphony No. 1 in C Major, op. 21, I, mm. 285–98; (*c*) Schubert, Symphony No. 4 in C Minor, D. 417, IV, mm. 475–86.

series of cadences is over (2.8*a*) or the composing-out of the tonic chord is finished (2.8*b* and 2.8*c*). Listeners accept the reiterated tonic chords as a satisfactory final closing gesture primarily because they conform to gestures that end other movements

EXAMPLE 2.8 (*cont.*)

known to them. Thus, because of conformant relationships the first two tonic chords imply that a final, third tonic chord will conclude the movement.

Inter-opus conformant relationships are not restricted to brief, formulaic patterns. Such patterns are simply the most common, no doubt because compact formulas are easier to remember. Larger conventional formal designs can also imply a more or less specific point of conclusion.

Consider the classical da capo aria. As experienced listeners, we know that the typical da capo aria will be in overall three-part form, ABA. Whatever closure exists at the end of the second A section is strengthened by the fact that it is a return of familiar music. The performer may reinforce the closure of the second A section by slowing down or otherwise differentiating it from the initial statement, but that is not necessary since once we recognize that the work is a da capo aria, we expect it to conform to other da capo arias we have heard. Hence we fully expect the aria to conclude at the end of the second statement of A.

All kinds of conformant relationships—intra-opus, inter-opus, those that relate brief gestures, and those that relate large-scale formal designs—can help, then, to imply a specific point of conclusion. The ability to enhance closure results from the return of a passage within a work, or the repetition of a closing gesture or formal design from other works familiar to the listener.

Conformant relationships are formal relationships in that events are considered synchronically and treated as separate entities. Events and elements can also be related to one another through processes that occur over time. Such processes involve changes within individual parameters. Changes that result in directed motion can be ordered according to increasing tension or activity (intensifying changes), decreasing tension or activity (abating changes), or the rules of *syntax* (either intensifying or abating changes).

SYNTACTIC RELATIONSHIPS

Exactly how the word syntax should be used in connection with music needs to be discussed. In language, syntax is the way in which words are organized to form sentences. Words are classified according to their use, or function: proper noun, common noun, transitive verb, intransitive verb, adverb, and so on. Studying syntax involves finding "rules by which words and groups of words may be strung together to form grammatical sentences,"[33] such as:

article/common noun/transitive verb/article/common noun.

A grammatical sentence need not make any sense, however: "The book murdered the banana." is grammatically correct. The meanings of the individual words and how they cooperate to create the meaning of the sentence is a matter of semantics.

The clear-cut differentiation between syntactic form and semantic content does not, as a rule, apply in music. That is so because, unlike words, musical elements do not have any specific meaning outside of a given context. The word *banana* has meaning because it signifies something beyond itself: it refers to a specific kind of fruit. However, an isolated chord has only abstract signification; the chord can signify something precise only in a particular musical context.[34] In a piece of program music, for instance, the chord may come to signify a character, object, or event; or in a specific tonal context the chord may signify the tonic or subdominant or dominant (among other possibilities).

In music, then, what an element means depends upon its role in a string of elements. Musical syntax is the way in which musical elements are arranged to form coherent phrases, periods—in short, structures with the inherent quality of intelligible order. We become familiar with intelligible orders as we become familiar with a musical style. Thus syntactic relationships are style dependent. In language the existence of a semantic component allows the possibility of illogical or nonsensical meanings; in music this sort of nonsense cannot occur.[35] The rules of musical syntax establish possible orderings of musical elements through which the elements acquire meaning in their relationships to one another. For a parameter to be syntactic therefore, we must be able to perceive and relate discrete elements, and we must have rules that define closure and rules that define functional relationships between elements.[36]

In much of Western music, the only parameters that listeners typically and consistently segment into distinct elements are those that organize pitches or durations: tonal and registral pitch, harmony and concordance, and duration.[37] What often differentiates those parameters from others like dynamics and timbre is that each is based on a restricted set of distinct elements out of the available spectrum of elements. For example, the pitches used in most Western music are distinct because they are spaced rather far apart when one considers our remarkable ability to discriminate differences in pitch.[38] Therefore, changes in pitch, except for a rare portamento, are stepped changes; the smallest interval of change is usually a half step. On the other hand, Western composers commonly indicate gradual changes (crescendos and decrescendos) as well as stepped changes in dynamics. A crescendo or decrescendo represents a continuous segment of—not selected points from—the entire dynamic range. Hence the elements that make up a crescendo or decrescendo are not distinct.

Note that there is also an important difference between the way in which we segment parameters involving pitches and the way in which we segment the parameters of duration and rhythm. Discrete pitch elements are essentially constant from work to work, so that middle C in one piece is identifiably the same as middle C in another piece.[39] Not so with durations; we have no clear sense of what any particular duration is. The elements are distinct, but have only proportional values within a piece. For whatever reasons, we only perceive discrete, constant elements in the parameters of tonal and registral pitch, and in harmony and concordance.

In addition to being distinct, elements of a parameter must generally be separated by nonuniform intervals for syntax to exist.[40] A chromatic scale or a series of eighth notes does not provide an internal basis for defining closure or determining functional relationships. Since syntax involves the study of how musical elements are organized to form phrases and periods, we must have specific rules that define such structures. Consequently, criteria for closure must be constituted. Moreover, there must be rules for the ordering of elements within the phrase and period—rules that establish functional relationships among elements in particular arrangements. It is not sufficient to have well-defined criteria for closure. If elements can be arranged arbitrarily except at points of closure, syntax does not exist.

In some parametric processes and patterns, the lack of a specific point of termination usually precludes closure. With respect to dynamics, for instance, a crescendo does not imply a specific point of conclusion; it can stop or terminate, but it cannot close.[41] Similarly, what constitutes a specific conclusion for processes involving timbre is undefined. So it is, in general, for a series of abating durations, too. A string of increasing durations does not generally imply a specific conclusion, since the conclusion of the string comes with the longest duration in the string and we do not know what that will be.[42] That is, it is unclear from the durational process itself when it will conclude, though clues from other parameters may make it possible for us to predict with some confidence when it will end. With respect solely to the durations, however, only retrospectively (as in the case of a crescendo) do we recognize that a particular element terminated the process. Contrast that with the situation for the parameter of tonal harmony, in which the tonic is a specific goal of processes and typically serves as a point of closure. In general there is no corresponding durational, dynamic, or timbral "tonic" element.

A few parameters have specific points of termination because there is a distinct upper or lower limit to their range of possible elements. However, none of these parameters have rules for the ordering of elements within a phrase. For example, the parameter of *components*—the number of differentiated voices (lines) in a musical fabric—has a distinct lower limit of one component. Therefore, a process of diminishing components may be said to close at the point of reaching just one component. Nevertheless, we do not have rules for the ordering of components, so the parameter is not syntactic.

In tonal music, we can identify rules that define closure and rules that specify functional relationships between elements for parameters that are governed by tonality, which may be defined as a set of pitch relationships and functions based on a central point of reference—the tonic—to which all other elements are related. Moreover, those parameters have distinct elements that are separated by nonuniform intervals. Hence tonal pitch and harmony are syntactic parameters.[43] It is not clear that we have anything but the most rudimentary rules for the ordering of elements in parameters other than tonal ones. It is true that elements of the parameters of durations, dynamics, components, and timbre can be organized in an abating or intensifying series, in alternation, or kept constant,[44] but none of the parameters feature the rather complex set of functional relationships found in the syntactic parameters of tonal pitch and harmony. And not all of them have distinct elements and rules for closure. In this book, then, we will consider syntactic processes to arise from the parameters of tonal pitch and harmony.[45]

Major-minor tonality is an extremely complex subject which has been treated at length in numerous books, and it is not our intent to discuss more than its broadest outlines here. Of course major-minor tonality is based on a division of the octave into a series of whole steps and half steps that define major and minor modes. Chromatic pitches or harmonies are understood in relation to these diatonic elements, which are related to the tonic. For both tonal pitch and harmony, the tonic is a specific point of relative repose, though it is not always treated as such. Outside of these shared characteristics, tonal pitch and harmony differ in the ways elements are functionally related to the tonic.

As is well known, different degrees of the scale have different functions. The first degree is most stable, followed by the fifth and then the third degrees. A degree of closure is created when pitch patterns imply and reach the third or fifth degree,[46] though ultimate continuation to the tonic is implied. Pitch motion that produces the strongest tonal pitch closure will both imply and reach the tonic from the leading tone, the least stable scale degree.

Tonal harmony has to do with the relationships and functions of both intervals and chords, but primarily of chords. Of course, major and minor triads are the most stable because their intervals are the most consonant,[47] and a chord is most stable when it is in root position, and least stable when the lowest tone is the fifth of the chord.

Tonic, dominant, and subdominant functions and the basic principle of root movement by fifths provide the foundation for syntactic relationships between harmonies. Because of the syntactic rules, certain progressions are more probable than others. The existence of syntactic rules allows Walter Piston to list "a table of usual root progressions" in his textbook on harmony.[48] The table amounts to a description of the most common ways in which composers of tonal music realized the rules of harmonic syntax.

Harmonic closure in tonal music is created by various kinds of cadences, which were established through repeated use. The closural strength of a cadence depends on many different factors. A perfect authentic cadence is most powerful: $V_{(7)}$–I, both chords in root position and with the tonic in the highest voice of the I chord. The addition of a seventh to a dominant chord adds dissonant factors (the minor seventh between the root and seventh as well as the diminished fifth between the third and seventh) which strengthen the implication of motion to the tonic.[49] A common strong final cadence consists of ii_5^6 or IV followed by $(I_4^6-)V_7$–I, where the I_4^6 chord actually is a double appoggiatura on a dominant root. The conventional closing gestures shown in Example 2.7 end with such a cadence. Often a plagal cadence (IV–I) is used after an authentic cadence to confirm closure, especially at the end of a movement or work.

Not all cadences create strong closure, however. Deceptive cadences do not resolve to the implied tonic triad, so harmonic closure is temporarily avoided (though often the melody reaches closure). Some half cadences, which end on the dominant chord, are in a sense just incomplete authentic cadences; typical examples include the chord progressions $IV-I_4^6-V$, $ii_6-I_4^6-V$, and $vi-I_4^6-V$. Such chord progressions often serve to mark the end of a phrase, though closure may be more a result of rhythm and duration than harmony. The half cadence signifies closure, though closure of a weaker sort since it represents the completion of an *incomplete* passage. That is, a half cadence at the end of an antecedent phrase completes an incomplete musical statement that reaches harmonic closure with the authentic cadence that ends the consequent phrase. The half cadence produces relatively weak closure; the authentic cadence produces relatively strong closure.[50]

Other half cadences create harmonic closure because the dominant chord is implied as a local point of conclusion; examples are authentic cadences *on* the dominant (not *in* the dominant). With respect, however, to the entire period—that is, on a higher structural level—the dominant chord implies an ultimate resolution to the tonic.

Hierarchic structures are an important consequence of the existence of syntax.

EXAMPLE 2.9. Beethoven, Symphony No. 2 in D Major, op. 36, I, mm. 338–60.

EXAMPLE 2.9 (*cont.*)

They are possible because different degrees of closure are possible. Motives defined by provisional closure can combine to form phrases, which may be related together in higher-order patterns such as antecedent-consequent periods, rounded binary forms, and large-scale designs like sonata forms. There are, of course, a limited number of ways in which a composer can use tonal harmony alone to articulate the various levels of a hierarchic structure. Often the number of structural levels in a work exceeds the number of different cadences available to differentiate one structural level from another. Once a composer uses a perfect full cadence to close a process on a particular level, for example, what cadence remains that will provide stronger closure—strictly with respect to harmony—on a higher structural level?[51] In order to strengthen closure on the highest structural levels, composers of the eighteenth and early nineteenth centuries commonly repeated cadential formulas several times in succession. Thus, instead of a single perfect authentic cadence at the end of a closing section or coda, a composer would often write a series of perfect authentic cadences. Such passages, which are on some level a prolongation of the tonic, were frequently followed by reiterated tonic chords or a composing-out of the tonic chord.

Consider the end of the first movement of Beethoven's Symphony No. 2 in D Major, op. 36 (Example 2.9). Apparently a single perfect full cadence was not powerful enough to indicate the end of the movement, because there are four such cadences in the space of just thirteen measures: ii^6_5–V_7–I cadences are found in measures 338–40, 343–44, 347–48, and 349–50, followed by ten measures emphasizing the tonic chord. The reiterated cadences create an open, additive structure on the level of the individual cadences. Each cadence is closed, but from the standpoint of harmony the series of cadences lacks closure because the cadences are essentially identical. No ongoing harmonic process implies that the series will terminate with the cadence in measures 349–50. In cases such as this, listeners are aware that the movement is ending, but are unsure which cadence will be the last unless some process in another parameter clearly differentiates one of the cadences from the others. In Example 2.9 the durational patterning produces strong closure that reinforces the harmonic repose in measure 350. The tutti tonic octaves in measure 350 are sustained for three beats, thereby creating durational repose after the eighth- and sixteenth-note motion at the end of measure 349. In contrast, throughout measures 338–40 a steady stream of eighth notes in the low strings prevents strong durational closure. After the tonic chord is prolonged in measures 350–54, it is emphasized by alternating tonic and dominant chords in measures 354–58. Then the movement closes with a variation of the conventional closing gesture illustrated in Example 2.8—that is, three tonic chords, this time with the third chord extended. Strong durational closure occurs in measure 360, where the *compound duration*—a composite of concurrent durations—is the longest in the movement. Moreover, the fortissimo tonic octaves recall the practically identical sonorities that began the movement. Thus, conformant relationships and durational patterning are crucial in producing final closure.

In hierarchic music, closure is relatively stronger at the ends of phrases that complete one or more higher-level processes. For instance, if a phrase that ends with a perfect authentic cadence in the dominant is followed by a phrase that ends with a perfect authentic cadence in the tonic, the latter phrase has especially strong closure since the concluding tonic chord completes a higher-level V–I process between phrases.[52] Nevertheless, one must be careful to avoid placing too much importance on the closure of high-level syntactic processes. Sometimes an emphasis on harmony as *the* force for creating closure on all structural levels has obscured the critical role played by other parameters. That is especially evident in the work of Schenkerian analysts, who overemphasize the closure of high-level syntactic processes and tend to ignore secondary parameters.[53]

Consider the coda in the first movement of Beethoven's "Eroica" Symphony; the final measures (670–91) are shown in Example 2.10. According to Schenker's analysis,[54] the movement closes at measure 547, the point at which $\hat{1}$ arrives and all tensions cease. Schenker considered the rest of the movement a prolongation of that conclusion, and on the highest structural level it is. However, there is a shift from E♭ major to C major in measure 561, and then C major is treated as the dominant of F minor. The temporary changes in tonal center create harmonic tension that is not completely resolved until the perfect full cadence in E♭ major at measures 625–31.[55] The movement is far from over, though. E♭ major is prolonged for 60 measures (to the end of the movement) in large part by alternating tonic and dominant harmonies.

Why does the movement end after the perfect authentic cadence in measures 688–89 and not after the cadential resolution in measure 547, 631, 647, 655, 673, or 677? (The latter two cadences are shown in Example 2.10.) What, if anything, differentiates the resolution at measure 689? Is the final cadence a real conclusion or merely a termination?

EXAMPLE 2.10. Beethoven, Symphony No. 3 in E♭ Major, op. 55 ("Eroica"), I, mm. 670–91.

To answer those questions, we must go beyond Schenkerian analysis and consider secondary parameters and conformant relationships. Experienced listeners will expect final closure to occur in a way that conforms to other fast movements by Beethoven. In his style, fast movements almost always end with a tutti fortissimo tonic chord whose notes are the same duration in all parts.[56] The first movement of the "Eroica" ends that way, and an examination of the coda reveals that these features of dynamics and duration are what distinguish the cadence in measures 688–89 from the others.

Final closure is avoided in measures 543–47 and following in two ways: (1) there is only a *forte* tonic resolution of a *fortissimo* dominant seventh chord, and (2) in measure 551 the final tutti chord on the tonic is elided with a new phrase in the strings. Furthermore, measures 547–52 conform to the final measures of the exposition, so the listener familiar with Beethoven's style anticipates that a coda, not final closure, will follow. The harmonic return to E♭ major at measure 631 is weakened by its piano dynamic level and its elision with the next phrase in the first horns and violins. Similarly, none of the next five cadences (at measures 638–39, 646–47, 654–55, 670–73, and 676–77) brings final closure because the tonic resolutions are not fortissimo; moreover, except for measures 670–73, the durational patterning does not support closure.

A clearly discernible process of increasing dynamic levels in measures 631–73 implies that final closure will come with the cadence in measures 670–73, given in Example 2.10. Shortly before the excerpt begins, the dynamic level is increased by the addition of more and more components in measures 631–47. A crescendo begins in measure 647 and reaches fortissimo in measure 671, where a I^6_4 chord implies a cadence I^6_4–V_7–I. After the V_7 in measure 672, the listener expects the fortissimo tonic resolution that was avoided back in measure 547 (at the end of the recapitulation). The resolution of the perfect full cadence in measures 670–73 fails to bring final closure, however, because the tonic chord arrives *piano*, with reduced orchestration, and is elided with another phrase.

A crescendo beginning in measure 677 leads back to the fortissimo dynamic level at measure 685. Again the fortissimo coincides with a chord of dominant function (compare measure 546 as well as 571–72). Again the listener expects a fortissimo tonic resolution. This time the expectation is realized, and the movement closes with reiterated tonic chords in measures 689–91 (a composing-out of the concluding tonic chord).

Thus, examination of closure in the first movement of the "Eroica" reveals that secondary parameters can be a very real force in articulating, as well as reinforcing or weakening, closure produced by syntactic parameters. Harmony and tonal pitch are clearly the most important parameters affecting closure in tonal music, but other parameters play a significant role. As we observed earlier, closure is a relative condition whose strength is increased to the extent that secondary parameters support the process of abatement. Ignoring the effects of secondary parameters on closure results in biased, incomplete analyses.

*   *   *

We have briefly considered two of the three ways in which musical elements can be related to one another, by conformance and in a syntactic process, and how those relationships can contribute to producing or enhancing closure. We now turn to an examination of how musical elements can be arranged in processes of intensification or abatement in secondary parameters, and how those relationships affect closure.

CHAPTER 3

Secondary Parameters and Closure

Concentrated attention on the parameters of tonal pitch and harmony in tonal music has led to the development of rather sophisticated theories and methodologies for those parameters. We have yet to establish any substantial theory and methodology for secondary parameters. In recent years theorists who do recognize the importance of secondary parameters have tended to discuss them in an *ad hoc* manner or to concentrate their attention on one or two.[1] Many of these same writers have drawn their musical examples largely from tonal music, in which the primary parameters are of overriding concern.[2] What we need is a theory of secondary parameters that enables us to understand how they can function in both tonal and nontonal music.

Presumably some secondary parameters become primary parameters in nontonal music, since tonal pitch and harmony are not operative. In this study, though, we are primarily concerned with closure in tonal music, so I will continue to refer to registral pitch, concordance, dynamics, duration, timbre, and components as secondary parameters.

Perhaps the biggest problem in studying secondary parameters is the absence of any consistent and generally accepted set of concepts.[3] At least four factors contribute to the problem: (1) the imprecise use of the term *parameter,* (2) the ambiguous nature of some current terminology, (3) the occasional confusion of acoustical and psychological terms, and (4) the lack of accepted technical terms for some secondary parameters. We will discuss each of these in turn.

Indiscriminate use of the term parameter in writings on music has obscured a useful distinction between more or less *in*dependent variables on the one hand, and dependent variables on the other. Dynamics and rhythm, for instance, are often called parameters since they are variables in music. Yet dynamics (the relative loudness of sounds) is a more or less independent variable, whereas rhythm (which has to do with grouping sounds into patterns where unaccented beats are related to accented ones) is a dependent variable determined by a number of interacting parameters such as harmony, pitch, duration, and dynamics. Therefore, rhythm may be considered a summarizing property, an *emergent property,* which may be defined as a variable of music that is essentially dependent on two or more independent variables.[4] The focus of this study is on those variables in music that may be considered more or less independent, and hereafter the term parameter will be reserved for those variables, including dynamics. Other, dependent variables of music will be referred to as emergent properties. It follows that the primary independent variables—the primary parameters—of tonal music are tonal pitch and harmony.

A second problem is the ambiguity of terms such as texture. It is not always clear what aspect of texture a writer has in mind. Is texture characterized by the number of voices, as when we say that a piece has a three-voice texture? Or does it refer to the ways in which we perceive components, for example, as a figure with a ground (homophonic) or as a set of concurrent figures (polyphonic)? Does it indicate the tone color of a sound, as when a passage is said to have a light or heavy texture? Or does it denote the spacing of the components, as when we speak of a thin or thick texture? Or does texture simply refer to the arrangement of components at a specific moment in time?[5] Unfortunately, the answer to all of these questions is yes, depending on the context. Obviously a term such as texture can be a source of confusion unless it is carefully defined and consistently applied.

In this study, texture refers to the ways in which we organize musical stimuli into a ground alone, a figure or figures with a ground, or concurrent figures.

In any discussion of musical parameters it is important to establish whether one is talking about physical or psychological parameters. Frequency and intensity, for instance, are acoustical terms for physical parameters of sound. Such parameters have values that can be measured precisely and expressed numerically. However, music is the result of cognitive experience rather than a succession of physical stimuli, so our concern in this study is with psychological parameters, such as registral pitch (that is, those aspects of pitch that are independent of tonality) and dynamics. It is important to realize that "seeing, hearing, and remembering are all acts of construction, which may make more or less use of stimulus information depending on circumstances."[6] Accordingly, from this point on parameter will refer to a *psychological* parameter.

Our perceptions of pitch and other parameters are a result of cognitive processes and are not susceptible to direct physical measurement and precise quantification.[7] We do not, for example, tend to associate specific numbers with individual pitches; rather we perceive pitches as being higher or lower on a psychological scale. In general, a listener can judge whether two perceptions of a secondary parameter are equal or one is greater (or higher) than the other.[8] Beyond such basic determinations, we are not equipped to make precise quantitative judgments of, for example, how much higher one pitch is than another or how much greater one dynamic level is than another unless we have a mental concept of a fundamental unit of measurement (such as the half step in pitch or the basic pulse in duration). When we lack such a mental concept—as is generally the case with respect to dynamics, for instance—the best we can do is make quite vague quantitative comparisons like "twice as loud."[9]

A fourth factor contributing to the confusion surrounding secondary parameters in music is the fact that we have no generally accepted technical terms for some of them. The deficiencies in terminology become obvious if one considers the secondary parameters in monophonic music and then in homophonic or polyphonic music. There are four secondary parameters in monophonic music: *registral pitch, dynamics, duration,* and *timbre.* Those parameters are associated, respectively, with the four physical attributes of a musical stimulus: its fundamental frequency, intensity, physical duration, and spectrum. The same four secondary parameters are also found in music of more than one voice. In monophonic music the parameters define the linear succession of elements in one voice, and in homophonic or polyphonic music the parameters define not only the linear succession of elements in a single voice, but also the linear succession of *concurrent* elements in all voices.

We may say that in homophonic and polyphonic music, unlike monophonic, there are *compound elements,* which are the smallest definable values that relate combinations of musical stimuli. For example, a given pitch will help determine the form of a linear pitch pattern, comprised of simple elements, as well as the chordal structure, comprised of compound elements. In this study *registral pitch* is the secondary parameter that defines linear pitch patterns without regard to tonal function or significance. *Concordance* will refer to the secondary parameter that defines combinations of pitches without regard to tonal function or significance.[10]

Although harmony is a well-established term referring to differentiated concurrent pitches, there are no generally accepted terms that describe differentiated concurrent durations, dynamics, or timbres. This deficiency in terminology is indicative of the fact that secondary parameters have not received adequate attention in theory and analysis. In the interest of simplicity, I will use the terms *compound duration, compound dynamics,* and *compound timbre* for the secondary parameters that define differentiated concurrent durations, dynamics, and timbres, respectively.

Consider the general trends in the parameters of compound durations, compound dynamics, and compound timbres in Example 3.1. One arrives at a series of compound durations by taking the shortest duration in any part at a given point in time. That is, the overall series of attack points in all parts defines a series of durations which are compound durations. Accordingly, the compound durations in measures 155–57 are all eighth notes and the compound duration in measure 158 is a quarter note. Compound dynamics and compound timbres are summarizations of the dynamic levels and timbres, respectively, of all the components at a given point in time, in the same sense that statisticians average different elements to come up with an underlying trend. What is important is the general trend over a period of time, not the specific increase or decrease from one moment to another. There is an increase in compound dynamics at the beginning of measure 155 because the crescendos in the violins and flutes in the first two beats of the measure more than compensate for the diminishing dynamics in the bassoons and timpani. The compound dynamic level is reduced in the last part of measure 155 and throughout measure 156 because of the diminishing dynamics in the first violins and timpani (measures 155–56), bassoons

EXAMPLE 3.1. Mahler, Symphony No. 7, III, mm. 155–58. Used by permission of G. Schirmer, Inc. on behalf of the copyright owners, Bote & Bock.

(measure 155), and oboes (measure 156). Moreover, the second violins and then the bassoons and flutes drop out in measures 155–56. The fortissimo entrance of the bass clarinet in measure 157 results in a sudden increase in compound dynamics, which are reduced when the oboe reaches piano and then drops out in measure 157. Overall, the compound timbre changes from a very complicated mixed timbre incorporating some very bright tone colors (produced by the violins and oboes) to the relatively dull timbre of the solo bass clarinet.

Together with concordance, the parameters of compound duration, compound dynamics, and compound timbre will be referred to collectively as the *compound* secondary parameters. Accordingly, the other, *simple* secondary parameters will be called *simple duration, simple dynamics, simple timbre,* and *registral pitch.* Reference to both simple and compound duration will be made by using the word duration. Similarly, dynamics will refer to both simple and compound dynamics, and timbre to both simple and compound timbre.

The only remaining secondary parameter is *components,* the number of identifiable and differentiated strata in the musical fabric. Each of the components in homophonic or polyphonic music can theoretically be described in terms of the simple secondary parameters. In practice, however, the listener perceives individual components and cognitively summarizes them by grouping together the less well shaped (weaker and more uniform) components as an accompaniment, or ground, and the more well shaped patterns as figures. That is, the components that make up the ground tend to lose their individual identities, so it is probably inappropriate to analyze each in terms of the simple secondary parameters. Such an analysis is only appropriate for figures, which are uniquely defined by those four parameters, and the ground as a whole.

Several other variables frequently referred to as parameters are really emergent properties of music—summarizing properties essentially dependent on primary or secondary parameters. They are *meter, tempo, texture,* and *volume.* Each of these merits brief consideration.

Meter is not an independent variable that can be changed simply by replacing the notated time signature with a different one. Indeed, the time signature and bar lines may or may not indicate the actual meter—that is, the listener's perception of meter. Our perception of meter is dependent on more or less regularly recurring accents in a series of pulses.[11] Therefore, meter is dependent on the interaction of all parameters that create accented pulses, most notably the parameters of harmony, tonal pitch, registral pitch, compound duration, and compound dynamics.[12]

The listener's perception of tempo, sometimes referred to as "psychological tempo" or pace, can vary considerably from the notated tempo. Psychological tempo depends in part on the actual lengths of durations in a given performance, and in part on the rate of speed of a metrical unit, which in tonal music, at least, is chiefly defined by the primary parameters. That is, psychological tempo is slower or faster depending upon how durations are grouped in metrical units. For example, although the eighth notes in two pieces may be played at the same absolute speed, if one piece is in $\frac{3}{4}$ meter and the other in $\frac{6}{8}$ meter, of course the piece in triple meter will seem faster because the metrical unit is a quarter note rather than a dotted quarter note. Moreover, psychological tempo often varies in the same tonal piece depending upon the rate at which the underlying harmonies change. See, for instance, the increase in psychological tempo that takes place at measure 15 in the opening movement of Beethoven's *Sonate pathétique.*

Texture has to do with the ways in which the listener organizes the music into a ground alone, a figure or figures with a ground, or concurrent figures. What constitutes a ground or a figure, however, depends upon the interaction of many different parameters, including tonal pitch and harmony, registral pitch, concordance, and simple duration and timbre.

Volume, which is *not* used here to mean dynamics or intensity, may be used to refer to our perception of the size or "spaciousness" of a sound source—that is, how large or small a sound seems. Volume is an emergent property because it is entirely dependent on the registral pitch, dynamic level, and tone color of a sound. If other parameters remain constant, a lower registral pitch is greater in volume than a higher registral pitch, in part because lower registral pitches tend to have more audible overtones than higher registral pitches. Similarly, a louder sound is greater in volume than a softer sound, and a fuller tone, as determined by the greater number and strength of upper partials, is greater in volume than a thinner tone.

*   *   *

Now we will turn to a discussion of each secondary parameter and the ways in which processes in each parameter can enhance (that is, contribute to) and actually create closure.

Registral Pitch

Registral pitch is the simple parameter whose elements are the tones that define pitch patterns without regard to tonal function or significance. In the primary parameter of tonal pitch, pitches are organized in relationship to the tonic and the tonic is typically a stable goal of processes and patterns, but in registral pitch, on the other hand, the pitches are only organized along a linear scale from low to high (and vice versa), and no pitch has a privileged status as a stable goal. Moreover, the linear scale of registral pitch usually lacks clearly defined endpoints, which otherwise might serve as specific goals of processes and patterns. In order for a process or pattern in registral pitch to imply a particular point of conclusion, then, the process or pattern usually must either imply a return to a specific pitch or, owing to the phenomenon of octave equivalence, imply motion to an octave of a specific pitch. That is, because pitches that are an octave apart belong to the same class and are considered in some sense equal, an octave of a specific pitch may be a relative point of repose because in a way it represents a return to or attainment of the specific pitch in question. It should be said that what notes are perceived as beginning or ending a process or pattern in registral pitch actually depends in part on other parameters, in particular durations, since we perceive registral pitch in an overall musical context. Our focus at this time, though, is with those processes and patterns in registral pitch that might lead to closure.

Registral pitch patterns are characterized by the direction and size of the intervals between successive pitches,[13] and the pitch level (high or low) of the pattern. Each of these characteristics affects closure.

The direction of the intervals between pitches can have an important influence on closure. Ascending patterns tend to be intensifying, because we associate them with a sense of striving and effort—the greater the intervallic distance between pitches, the more the effort. That sense of effort may have to do with our personal experience in singing ascending leaps or even performing them on a wind instrument. Whatever the origin of the association, it seems to be widespread. Moreover, rising lines are often performed with a crescendo, or at least are perceived as increasing in loudness, which contributes to their tensive quality; see the discussion of dynamics below. No doubt we are all aware of the tendency of composers to use an ascending sequence to build to a climax and the tendency of performers to perform an ascending sequence with increasing loudness.

EXAMPLE 3.2. (*a*) Bach, Fugue in Bb Minor from *Das Wohltemperierte Clavier,* Book 1, mm. 7–12; (*b*) Brahms, Symphony No. 3 in F Major, op. 90, I, mm. 220–24.

In Example 3.2*a* the repetition of a motive at increasingly higher pitch levels builds tension.[14] The symbol I↗ indicates an intensification. Within each five-note pattern (shown in the second stave) there is a slight intensification, and underlying the ascending sequence are two ascending fourths (shown in the second and third staves) which are intensifying.

On the other hand, we generally associate a sense of relaxation with a descending pitch pattern, especially if it is conjunct.[15] Example 3.2*b* shows the conclusion of the first movement of Brahms's Third Symphony, where the repetition of a descending pitch pattern enhances closure.[16] Because of the conformant patterning, the F in measure 224 is an anticipated point of relative repose.

Psychologically, we tend to hear each pitch in a descent as moving *from* the previous one, whereas in an ascent we tend to hear each pitch as moving *toward* the next pitch.[17] As Robert Erickson says: "Put musically, movement upward is felt as strain, tension, lifting against a downward pull. Phrases push upward to a high point, then move downward to a lower point of relative relaxation and rest. . . . *We* push to the high note; *we* skip, slide, or fall to a lower note."[18] Descent, then, can be a sign of closure.

Our association of relaxation with descending pitch seems to come easily and naturally, and is found in speech as well as in music. Consider our inflection of speech: we raise our voice at the end of a question, and lower our voice at the end of a declarative sentence, especially so if the sentence completes a paragraph or other, higher level in the structural hierarchy. Raising one's voice for a question implies continuation—an answer should follow—and lowering one's voice at the end of a sentence implies completion and closure.[19] Similarly in music, ascending pitch patterns are generally intensifying and tend to imply continuation, whereas descending pitch patterns are abating and tend to imply closure.[20]

EXAMPLE 3.3. Bartók, *Concerto for Orchestra,* I, mm. 1–6. Copyright 1946 by Hawkes & Son (London) Ltd.; copyright renewed 1973. Reprinted by permission of Boosey & Hawkes, Inc.

In Example 3.3, for instance, an intensifying ascent is immediately followed by an abating descent. The symbol A⤵ indicates an abatement (it will be remembered that V^7 indicates an intensification). In measure 6 of Example 3.3 the return to C♯, which is an implied goal of the descending pitch pattern, creates registral pitch closure not only because it is a point of comparative repose following tension, but also because it represents a return to the initial pitch of a pattern—a pattern of intensification and abatement familiar to all of us, and one that may be found at all hierarchic levels in music.

In Example 3.4 an intensifying conjunct ascent is followed by an abating,

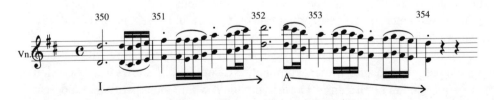

EXAMPLE 3.4. Beethoven, Symphony No. 2 in D Major, op. 36, I, mm. 350–54.

conjunct descent. Because of the privileged status of the octave, the D in measure 352 can be heard as the implied goal of the ascent that began with the D in measure 350. Therefore, even though the ascent is intensifying, there is a degree of registral pitch closure—which is supported by durational closure—with the arrival at D in measure 352. The closure in measure 352 is relatively weak, however, compared to the closure on the D in measure 354, where again closure is enhanced by the durational patterning on the lowest level. The D in measure 354 is a point of greater repose in part because it returns to the D of measure 350 and in part because it is comparatively more restful, coming as it does at the end of a process of intensification and abatement.

The size of the intervals between pitches can also have an important influence on closure. Disjunct pitch patterns, except for triadic ones, are usually more tensive than conjunct pitch patterns, because large intervals between pitches typically produce a sense of incompleteness that can only be totally resolved by a fill in the opposite direction from the disjunct interval. What constitutes a disjunction or *gap* in a pattern, and what constitutes a fill, will vary from culture to culture and style to style, depending on the size of the intervals used in the composition. In tonal music, any interval larger than a whole step can be heard as a gap that implies a subsequent conjunct fill, though tonal pitch patterns that are triadic or include an octave leap do not necessarily imply a conjunct fill, nor does an anacrusis that skips to the tonic a fourth above.[21] In general, the greater the gap between pitches, the more strongly some kind of fill is implied, but at some point a threshold is passed and the pitches will seem to be separate enough that no fill is anticipated.

Often a composer will use a disjunct, ascending pitch pattern to build to a climax. In the third movement of his Fourth Symphony (Example 3.5), Mahler builds to a local climax by using ever larger ascending leaps, "stretching" the initial D5-F5 gap in both directions until the final gap extends almost two octaves (A4-G#6).[22] Each ascending leap in Example 3.5 is more intensifying than the last.

EXAMPLE 3.5. Mahler, Symphony No. 4 in G Major, III, mm. 205–9.

Closure can be produced when a gap is filled in, thereby creating a "gap-fill" structure, not only because there is a return to the initial pitch of the pattern, but also because the return is a point of relative repose that completes a process implied by the initial gap. In a theme from the second movement of Mozart's Piano Concerto No. 23 in A Major, K. 488, the ascending leap from C# to A implies a descending fill (Example 3.6a). The symbol ⟼ means *implies,* and ⟩—⟶ means *realized.*[23]

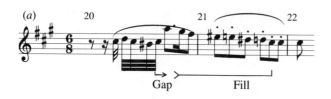

EXAMPLE 3.6. (a) Mozart, Piano Concerto No. 23 in A Major, K. 488, II, mm. 20–22; (b) Schubert, Symphony No. 8 in B Minor, D. 759, I, mm. 44–47.

Registral pitch closure is created with the return of C♯ in measure 21 because it completes a conjunct fill in the gap-fill structure. The conjunct, descending fill in Mozart's theme is relaxing and therefore strengthens the registral pitch closure on C♯ in measure 21.

Structural gaps are not always followed immediately by a fill, of course. In Example 3.6b the fill of the initial descending gap is somewhat delayed. With regard to the parameter of registral pitch, the G in measure 47 is closed because it concludes a conjunct fill of the initial G to D gap. If the fill of a structural gap is greatly delayed, closure may not be created because the implications of a fill may have been forgotten by the listener.

With respect to the size and direction of intervals between pitches, the strongest closure will come with the descending, conjunct return to the initial pitch of an ascending leap, as in the return to C♯ in Mozart's theme.

The pattern of ascending gap and descending fill, of tension followed by release, is typical of phrases in tonal music. Consider Example 3.7. A disjunct pitch pattern in the first two measures is followed by a conjunct fill in the next two measures, and the same organization is found in measures 5–8. Note that not all of the structural gaps have a subsequent fill. After eight measures the pattern is still incomplete because gaps from D4 to F4 in measure 1 and G4 to B♭4 in measure 5 have not been filled. However, the larger, and therefore more intensifying, gaps from F4 to B♭4 and B♭4 to E♭5 are followed by conjunct descents filling in the gaps. Of those fills, the latter is more complete because the descent returns to the initial pitch of the gap, B♭4.

Except for the difference in endings, the pitch pattern in measures 1–4 of Example 3.7 is repeated at a higher pitch level in measures 5–8. The fact that the four-measure patterns differ in pitch level affects our response to them, for generally

EXAMPLE 3.7. Schumann, *An den Sonnenschein,* op. 36, no. 4, mm. 1–8.

EXAMPLE 3.8. Schumann, *Dichterliebe,* op. 48, no. 7 (*Ich grolle nicht*), mm. 1–12.

speaking we find higher registers more tensive than lower registers in a given instrument or voice.[24] For instance, the leap of a perfect fourth up to E♭5 in measure 6 is slightly more tensive than the corresponding leap to B♭4 in measure 2. Composers often repeat pitch patterns at higher pitch levels as an intensification or at lower pitch levels as an abatement. In Example 3.8 the ascending pitch pattern in measures 5–6 is reiterated at a higher pitch level in the following two measures as part of an overall intensification in measures 5–8. The ascending leaps contribute to the tensive quality of the measures. However, the descending, conjunct line in measures 9–10 helps resolve the tension by providing a relaxing downward motion and a fill of the gap created in measure 7. The repetition of the descending third in measures 11–12 further enhances the abatement, and registral pitch closure is created by the return to E4, which completes the fill of the initial E4 to B4 gap.

Consider, too, the second movement of Beethoven's Seventh Symphony. At the beginning of the movement, the theme is played by the violas and subsequently repeated three times, each time an octave higher. At the end of the movement (measures 255–62 and again in 263–70), however, the theme is broken up into two-measure segments, each of which is played an octave lower than the previous one to create a closing gesture.

Many times in works by Mahler there is a registral gap between a high figure (or figures) and an underlying pedal. Sometimes one or more descending pitch patterns fill in the gap, and registral pitch closure is produced when the descending pitch pattern reaches the same registral pitch as the pedal. In Example 3.1, for instance, there is a D2 pedal in the timpani in measures 155–56 and very high pitch patterns in the flutes, oboes, and violins in measure 155. Descending pitch patterns in measures 155–57 lead to registral pitch closure on D2 in measure 158. At other times the descending pitch pattern does not arrive at the registral pitch of the pedal, but rather ends on an octave above the pedal. In such cases, there is a degree of registral pitch closure, since any octave of the pedal—which serves as a point of reference—is an implied point of relative repose. Thus, there is registral pitch closure on D4 in the oboe at measure 157 of Example 3.1. Registral pitch closure is stronger when the descending pitch pattern reaches the registral pitch of the pedal, however.

With regard to registral pitch, then, ascending sequences of the same or conformant motives tend to be intensifications. Descending sequences of the same or conformant motives are generally abatements.[25] Closure is created when a registral pitch pattern or process implies and reaches a particular pitch, or in some cases owing to the privileged status of the octave, reaches an octave of a particular pitch. The strongest such closure is created by the descending, conjunct return to the initial pitch of an ascending leap.

CONCORDANCE

Concordance is the compound parameter whose elements are combinations of pitches that define harmonic progressions without regard to tonality but rather with respect to the agreement between adjacent partials in the combined harmonic spectrum. Such progressions may be ordered according to processes of increasing concordance (abating processes) or decreasing concordance (intensifying processes) as shown, for instance, in Example 3.9. Whether we agree on the specific rank order of concordant intervals given in the example is not especially important, since our chief interest here is with perceptible trends in concordance—with processes of generally increasing or decreasing concordance—rather than with specific moment-to-moment judgments of

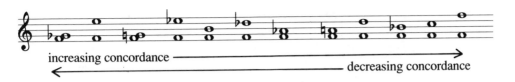

EXAMPLE 3.9. Varying degrees of concordance.

the relative concordance of adjacent harmonies. In this book I am using Hermann Helmholtz's rank ordering of just intervals given in Example 3.9 as a general guide to the relative concordance of harmonies.[26]

Note that I am using concordance to refer to the entire spectrum of harmonies, which range in concordance from high (most concordant) to low (discordant). Like loudness and softness or lightness and darkness, concordance and discordance are different aspects of the same quality. Therefore, the distinction between concords and discords is one of degree, not kind. Processes of decreasing concordance may also be described as processes of increasing discordance because both concordance and discordance are terms that refer to the relative smoothness (or roughness) of a harmony. Our perception of them is essentially a result of the physical attributes of harmonies rather than the syntactic relationships that arise in a particular tonal context.

In this study, then, concordance and discordance are distinguished from consonance and dissonance, which define the relative stability of chords in a tonal context.[27] The failure to make this distinction in the experimental literature has created a lot of confusion. That is, the term *consonance* has been used in the acoustical and psychoacoustical literature to refer both to what I am calling concordance and to what is generally called consonance by music theorists. Experimenters who presented subjects with paired intervals and asked them to make judgments of "consonance," then, were really asking subjects to judge which interval was more *concordant* rather than which was more consonant.[28] When Hermann Helmholtz explained the physical characteristics of sounds that contribute to our perception of concordance in 1863, his terms *Konsonanz* and *Dissonanz* referred to concordance and discordance, respectively, as defined above.[29]

As Helmholtz explained, and as recent researchers have confirmed, concordant harmonies are defined by the extent to which there is interference between pure-tone constituents—interference generally associated with rapid beats, which are fluctuations in the intensity of tones at regular intervals of time.[30] The roughness of harmonies is influenced by the number and relative intensities of concordant versus discordant upper partials.[31]

Our perception of concordance, then, is rooted in the very complicated physical characteristics of sounds. Presumably opinions may change over time about which sonorities are concords and which are discords, but the relative concordance of sonorities will not. It is impossible to define a specific rank ordering of harmonies from most concordant to least concordant, of course, but we may adopt a particular rank order of intervals as a general guide to distinguishing more concordant from less concordant harmonies. After all, in practice it is doubtful that listeners make clear distinctions between, for example, the concordance of a major sixth and a major third, or that of a minor third and a minor sixth. We need not agree, then, on the specific rank order of such intervals. I do assume, however, that listeners will find a major third inherently more concordant than, for instance, a minor seventh or a minor second.

Throughout Western music, concords generally have been used as consonances and discords as dissonances (though the perfect fourth is a notable exception). Since dissonances require resolution to consonances, there is a sense of tension associated with dissonances and a sense of repose associated with consonances. Hence, we associate tension and instability with discords not only because of their roughness, but also because of their use as dissonances.[32] Similarly, we associate repose and stability with concords because of their smoothness and also their use as consonances. With regard to the parameter of concordance, then, a pattern of decreasing concordance (increasing discordance) is an intensification and a pattern of increasing concordance is an abatement.

The unison and the octave, which are the most concordant of all harmonies, are two potential goals of processes or patterns that might create closure with respect to concordance. Three other potential points of closure in polyphonic or homophonic music are a perfect fifth, the most concordant dyad involving different notes, and a major or minor triad, the most concordant triads involving different notes. A passage may reach closure on one of the above-mentioned concords in a number of different ways. An abating process may lead to closure, or an intensifying process may lead to a reversal and resolution. It is not uncommon for a pedal tone in one or more voices to serve as a point of reference by which a particular concord is implied as a point of closure. Moreover, as with registral pitch, a process or pattern in concordance may suggest a particular point of conclusion by implying a return to a specific concord or, owing to the phenomenon of octave equivalence, by implying motion to an octave of a specific concord.

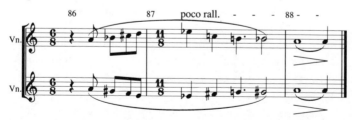

EXAMPLE 3.10. Bartók, *Music for Strings, Percussion and Celesta*, I, mm. 86–88. Copyright 1937 by Universal Editions; copyright renewed 1964. All rights reserved. Copyright and renewal assigned to Boosey & Hawkes, Inc., for the U.S.A. Reprinted by permission. Used by permission of European American Music Distributors Corporation, sole U.S.A. and Canadian agent for Universal Edition, for the territory of the world excluding the U.S.A.

In Example 3.10 there is a clearly discernible process of moving away from and subsequently back to the initial unison A. Strong concordant closure is created with the return of the unison A in measure 88, where of course durational closure supports final closure for the movement. Weaker concordant closure is created with the anticipated arrival at the octave E♭ in measure 87, where again durational patterning supports closure. Unisons and octaves tend to be used as goals of concordant processes and patterns in musical passages with only a few components.

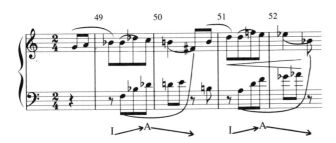

EXAMPLE 3.11. Hindemith, Piano Sonata No. 2, I, mm. 49–52. Copyright 1936 by B. Schott's Soehne, Mainz; copyright renewed. All rights reserved. Used by permission of European American Music Distributors Corporation, sole U.S.A. and Canadian agent for B. Schott's Soehne.

Whereas in Example 3.10 there is an alternation of relatively concordant and relatively discordant intervals, in Example 3.11 we find a series of intensifying and a series of abating concords. Constantly decreasing concordance in measure 49 ends with the major seventh on the last eighth note, at which point each successive simultaneity is more concordant. The short abatement leads to closure on the unison F♯ (note the phrasing mark in the left hand) in measure 50. The overall pattern of intensification followed by abatement is repeated at a higher pitch level in measures 51–52.

Strict processes of intensifying and abating concords such as that found in Example 3.11 are relatively rare. It may be that the general scarcity of sustained processes of increasing or decreasing concordance results from an avoidance of the most concordant sonorities in much of the music of the twentieth century, as well as an interest on the part of many composers to organize harmonies according to the syntactic rules of tonal harmony or following that model. That is, many composers of nontonal music have used the model of tonal harmonic progressions, which tend to grow in intensity toward a climax and then quickly resolve.[33]

One fairly common strategy of producing closure in tonal as well as nontonal music is to build up tension over a sustained pedal by using increasingly discordant harmonies, and then resolve to the triad whose root is the pedal tone, a specific point of relative repose implied by the pedal. For instance, in the third movement of Mahler's Second Symphony (Example 3.12), concordant closure occurs in measure 481 where a series of more or less discordant harmonies is resolved to a concord

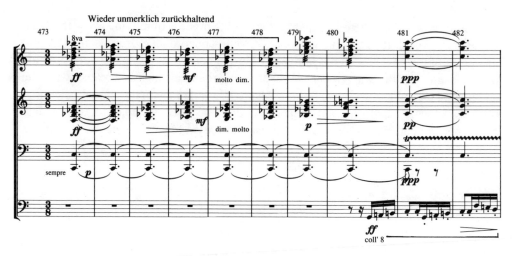

EXAMPLE 3.12. Mahler, Symphony No. 2, III, mm. 473–82.

consisting of doubled octaves and fifths built on the C pedal which had been sustained throughout measures 465–81. In addition to the pattern of concordance, the descending scalar pattern in the highest voice implies resolution to C.

SIMPLE AND COMPOUND DYNAMICS

Simple and compound dynamics are frequently strong factors in articulating closure in tonal music. They are the secondary parameters that define the loudness (or softness) of individual components and concurrent components, respectively.[34] Though it is difficult to specify simple or compound dynamics with precision, especially by looking at a musical score, listeners generally have little problem judging relative loudness and discerning patterns and processes in dynamics.[35] As with other secondary parameters, our concern here is primarily with overall trends in dynamics, rather than specific changes from moment to moment.

Elements of simple and compound dynamics often form patterns of increasing loudness (intensifying patterns) or decreasing loudness (generally abating patterns), as illustrated in Example 3.13. A diminuendo such as the one in Example 3.13 is particularly appropriate for shaping the end of a musical passage because we typically find soft sounds relaxing compared to loud sounds. (I say *typically* because there are situations in which the difficulty and effort of performing a very soft passage, such as a soprano's phrase on pianissimo high C, engenders tension and is not relaxing.) For the most part, though, we associate tension and strain with loud sounds, probably because of the great effort required to sing loud, scream, or play a loud sound on most instruments. Moreover, as noted earlier, there is a tendency for us to hear an ascending pitch pattern as increasing in loudness, and pitches in a high range as louder than pitches in a middle or low range.

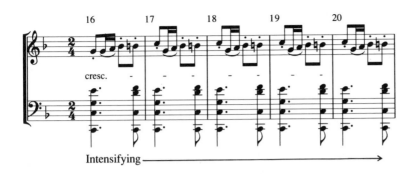

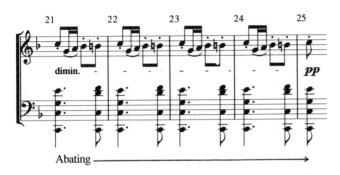

EXAMPLE 3.13. Beethoven, Symphony No. 6 in F Major, op. 68, I, mm. 16–25.

Simple and compound dynamics affect closure in the same ways. Both can help to articulate closure when a dynamic process implies and reaches an extreme dynamic level, either extremely loud or extremely soft. Generally speaking it is difficult for a process of intensifying or abating dynamics, in and of itself, to imply a particular point of conclusion, because there is no clearly defined loudest possible dynamic or softest possible dynamic. In practice, though, listeners make such judgments and determine that a given passage has reached the loudest or softest extreme in dynamics. Loud dynamic levels add a tensive quality to a conclusion, whereas soft dynamic levels enhance the repose of a conclusion. Both are effective because they differentiate a particular passage from others in the work.

Often an extreme level of loudness is used to give shape to a series of repeated cadences in tonal music. Indeed, because of the inherent tension in extremely loud sounds, loud conclusions such as the ending to Beethoven's "Eroica" (discussed in chapter 2) are possible because of decisive closure produced by some other parameter(s), especially the primary parameters, and because of stylistic convention. Repeating a cadence at a higher dynamic level emphasizes it and tends to make us believe that it is somehow more important than the previous one(s), even if the cadences are otherwise identical. The use of an extreme dynamic level for a particular cadence is a signal to the listener that the end has arrived—this cadence is the loudest, the most important, the last. By using a fortissimo level the composer introduces a tensive quality to the cadence, which creates an exciting conclusion rather than a truly restful one.

EXAMPLE 3.14. Schumann, *Kreisleriana,* op. 16, no. 8, mm. 139–45.

Abating dynamics often signal the end of a formal event, whose closure may be defined by some other parameter. Simple and compound dynamics enhance closure at the end of Schumann's *Kreisleriana* (Example 3.14). The perfect full cadence in measures 139–40 is exactly the same as those in measures 23–24 and 71–72 except for the decrescendo, which thereby differentiates this cadence and contributes to closure. The extension in measures 140–45 fades to an extreme dynamic level, *ppp*, approaching silence.[36] Thus, the music suggests that the D (representing the dominant) of measure 144 will be followed by a final, closing tonic (the G of measure 145).

EXAMPLE 3.15. Ives, Second Sonata for Violin and Piano, III (The Revival), conclusion. Copyright 1951 by G. Schirmer, Inc.; copyright renewed. International copyright secured. All rights reserved. Reprinted by permission.

Sometimes a concluding decrescendo follows the dynamic climax of the piece, as is shown in Example 3.15 from Ives's Second Violin Sonata. The *fff* level that begins the exerpt is the loudest in the work, after which the music fades to the softest dynamic level, *ppp*.[37] In this case the diminuendo is accompanied by a ritardando. Together these processes create the impression that the music is dying away, and that slowly the activity and tension in the music are waning.

Occasionally this concept is explicitly noted in the music, as when a composer

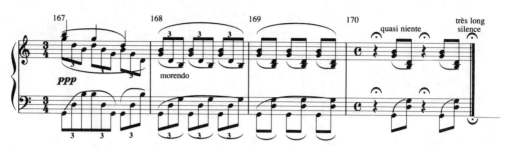

EXAMPLE 3.16. Liszt, *Apparitions No. 3: Fantaisie sur une valse de François Schubert*, mm. 167–70.

writes *morendo* ("dying") in the score. In Example 3.16 Liszt uses abating dynamics and durations to give shape to a concluding tonic chord, which eventually dies away. The use of rests in the last measure together with extremely soft dynamics enables Liszt to blur the boundary between the end of the music and the silence that usually acts as a "frame" separating a piece of music from its external environment. Especially in the late nineteenth century, such endings were not uncommon.

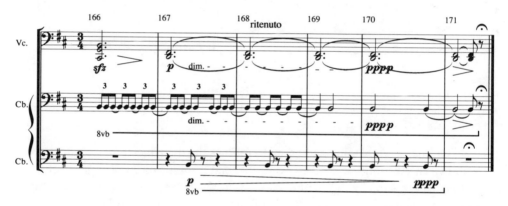

EXAMPLE 3.17. Tchaikovsky, Symphony No. 6 in B Minor, op. 74, IV, mm. 166–71.

In many instances it would seem that processes and patterns in the music imply that final closure will come only with the arrival of silence, as in Example 3.17 from the last movement of Tchaikovsky's Sixth Symphony. The tonic is prolonged throughout the coda of the movement (measures 147–71), which is characterized by a gradual reduction in components and diminishing dynamic levels. Final closure is created by the arrival of silence, a specific point of conclusion implied by the music, and enhanced by abating durations and unchanging harmony.[38]

The dynamic closure is all the more significant because the primary parameters remain unchanged in measures 167–71. In the absence of any ongoing processes in the primary parameters, the processes in the secondary parameters become more significant. If processes in the primary parameters were creating motion, then a decrescendo to silence would not produce satisfactory final closure unless abating motion in the primary parameters was terminally synchronized with the arrival of silence.[39]

SIMPLE AND COMPOUND DURATION

Simple and compound duration are the secondary parameters that define the durations (lengths in time) of simple elements and compound elements, respectively. Remember we are concerned with listeners' perceptions, so that durational lengths of simple and compound elements will be affected by tempo. Compound durations are created by the combination of simple durations, and are essentially determined by the series of intervals between attack points, as illustrated in Example 3.18.

EXAMPLE 3.18. Schoenberg, String Trio, op. 45, mm. 57–61.

Compound durational patterns are not always exactly the same as patterns of attack points, however. At times a significant and readily perceived change in the combined sonority, generally because one or more voices drop out, has the impact of an attack point and should be counted as defining an interval of compound duration. In Example 3.18, for instance, the rest at the beginning of measure 59 defines a compound duration, though it is not an attack point. Because the music suggests an underlying metrical structure, the listener probably perceives a "phantom" downbeat, perhaps only retrospectively, rather than a rest that in some sense prolongs the half notes at the end of measure 58. Another example of the difference between compound durations and attack point rhythms would have been provided by Example 3.18 if the violin's Ab in measure 61 had been sustained but not re-attacked on the second beat; the sudden reduction to a single component would have had an impact similar to that of an attack point on the second beat. One must deal with such cases on an individual basis, because whether an attack point is perceived depends on how sharply the sustained note is differentiated from the previous sonority.

Durational patterns differ from the pattern of attack points in at at least one other instance. With respect to both simple and compound durations, there are times when a trill or tremolo should be counted as an articulated durational pattern—when it grows out of increasing rhythmic activity—and other times when it can be ignored because it is an unmeasured articulation necessary, as in the timpani, to sustain a pitch.

Simple and compound durational patterns can be divided into three basic types: (1) additive durations such as ♩♩♩♩, (2) cumulative durations such as ♪ ♩ ♩, and (3) countercumulative durations such as ♩   ♩ ♫.[40] Each of these types warrants discussion.

Additive durations tend to promote mobility because they imply continuation of the pattern. They are especially common in compound durations, and they can lead to closure if the additive series leads to a longer duration, as in Example 3.18 where the compound durational pattern in measures 59–61 concludes on a dotted half note. A degree of stability, and hence a degree of repose, is created whenever a shorter note moves to a longer note, and the dotted half note in measure 61 is a point of repose relative to the preceding eighth notes. In other words, the dotted half note arrests the motion produced by the eighth notes. A degree of durational closure occurs the moment that the eighth-note duration is exceeded—that is, when the listener realizes that the duration is longer than the preceding one. The sense of durational closure is instantaneously implied and realized, and the state of relative repose continues for the length of the note.

Often a process or pattern in some other parameter implies a particular point of conclusion for an additive durational pattern. In Example 3.18, the reduction to A♭ in the violin at measure 61 is an implied point of closure for several reasons: the A♭ had been established as a point of closure by virtue of concluding the brief phrase in measures 57–58 (where it is written as G♯) and concluding a variation of the violin's four-note pattern which follows in measures 59–60 (where the whole-note duration enhances closure); moreover, the abrupt reduction to the A♭ in measure 60 marks the pitch in the listener's consciousness, and accordingly the listener probably anticipates that the reintroduction of a solo A♭ in measure 61 is likely to conclude the phrase.

Strictly additive durational patterns are generally quite brief in tonal music— except, perhaps, on higher structural levels—because the listener tends to perceive cumulative or countercumulative structures in additive patterns even when the durations are equally spaced. Experimental evidence shows that listeners are inclined to hear equally spaced sounds in groups of two or four, which probably reflects the influence of meter and the importance of cultural conditioning. Listeners perceive the interval between groupings as longer and the initial sound of each group as more intense even if the sounds are evenly spaced and of equal physical intensity.[41] In general, then, additive durations soon lead to either a longer or a shorter duration, thereby creating a cumulative or countercumulative durational pattern.

Cumulative durations are generally abating because they reduce activity (in the sense of attack points) and hence impede mobility. For instance, given the series of durations ♪ ♪ ♩ 𝅗𝅥, the quarter note is a point of repose relative to the preceding eighth notes, and the half note is a point of repose relative to the quarter note (as well as to the eighth notes). When the listener hears the two eighth notes followed by the quarter note rather than another eighth (or shorter) note, he or she recognizes that the quarter note is a point of relative repose, though the quarter note has the potential to be part of an ongoing abating process—especially since in general a quarter note is not a particularly long duration. If the quarter note is followed by a shorter note value, then retrospectively the listener knows that the quarter note was *not* part of a larger cumulative pattern but rather completed a cumulative durational pattern. Consequently, at least in the listener's mind, closure is enhanced.

If, on the other hand, the quarter note is followed by a half note, as in our example, then retrospectively the listener knows that the quarter note was part of an ongoing cumulative durational pattern that may (or may not) conclude with the half note. The half note is a point of durational closure and is the point of greatest repose because it is the longest in the series. Unless some other process or design implies that the half note completes the cumulative durational pattern, however, the listener may anticipate that the half note will be followed by an even longer duration, which would then be the greatest point of repose in the series. Theoretically any duration can always be followed by a longer duration, and the longest duration in a pattern will be perceived as the conclusion of the pattern.[42]

In practice, processes and patterns in other, especially primary, parameters guide the listener's judgments as to which duration will complete a cumulating durational process. Sometimes, too, a durational pattern has been established so the listener can anticipate closure with the arrival of the duration that previously ended the pattern. Also, the listener may decide that an extremely long note, such as 𝅝 (fermata), is so long that it must be the last note of a pattern, but when that decision can be made is unclear. Although it is evident that a series of cumulative durations create points of durational closure, the series *per se* does not usually imply a specific point of conclusion. One simply cannot define a point of greatest possible repose for processes in the parameters of simple and compound duration, as one can with the octave in concordance.

A cumulating durational pattern can create strong closure if it conforms to a previous pattern, because the repetition or return implies a specific ending point: the same duration that concluded the original statement of the pattern. That is illustrated in Example 3.19, where the rhythmic pattern ♫ ♫ ♩ ♪ in the melody in measures 5–6 (marked with a bracket) is repeated in measures 7–8. The listener probably will not expect that a longer duration will follow the eighth notes at the beginning of measure 6, since the first statement of the rhythmic pattern ♫ ♫ ♩ in measures 4–5 continues with eighth notes. Nevertheless, the listener no doubt will perceive the quarter note G in measure 6 as completing a cumulative durational pattern. Then the repetition of a conformant rhythmic pattern beginning in measure 7 implies that a quarter note will follow the final two eighth notes in measure 7.

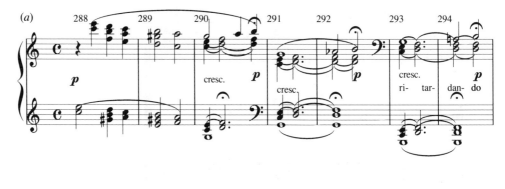

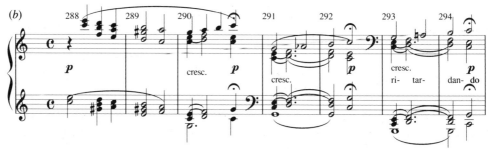

EXAMPLE 3.22. Beethoven: (*a*) Piano Sonata in C Major, op. 53, I ("Waldstein"), mm. 288–94; (*b*) recomposed version of (*a*).

Rests, like cumulative durations, can be abating or intensifying depending on the musical context as determined by the primary parameters. Rests following the passage given in Example 3.22*a,* for instance, would support the intensification of measures 290–94 by further delaying the greatly anticipated tonic resolution. Also, rests do not enhance repose if they clearly interrupt one or more processes in the primary parameters, as occurs in measures 45–46 of Haydn's Symphony in D Major, No. 104, third movement. However, rests that follow a cadence or other point of closure enhance closure since they separate the cadence from what follows—the longer the rests, the stronger the closure. Experiments by Idson and Massaro indicate that notes that are followed by rests are perceived as longer than notes of equal physical duration that are not followed by rests.[44] Therefore, if the chords in an authentic cadence are notated and played the same physical length but are followed by a rest, the tonic chord will be perceived as longer than the dominant chord. The result, then, would be a cumulative durational pattern.

Of course, performers can and do alter the physical length of chords or notes to weaken or emphasize closure. Often performers slow down at the ends of phrases, sections, and entire works, since cumulating durations are a sign of closure. In a study of durations in actual performances Alf Gabrielsson found that "A common type [of durational deviation] at the measure level can be described as a 'long-short-short-long' pattern over four measures, in other words, a 'slow start'—accelerating in the middle—retarding toward the end, an easily recognized type of phrasing in much music."[45]

Accelerating tends to produce *countercumulative* durations, which of course promote mobility. Composers commonly use an accelerando to create an intensification. Typically the performers are asked to increase speed throughout a designated passage, but occasionally the accelerando is actually composed out, as in measures 137–48 of the third movement of Beethoven's Piano Sonata in E Major, op. 109.[46] One can even end a work with an accelerando, but final closure is dependent on strong closure in other, usually primary, parameters.[47]

Although countercumulative durational patterns are usually intensifying, they may lead to a reversal and hence closure. That is, a final *cumulating* duration may conclude a passage characterized by generally countercumulative durations, much as an intensifying harmonic process leads to a climax on the dominant which is resolved directly to a concluding tonic. In fact such primary parametric closure usually accompanies a countercumulative durational pattern that ends with a cumulating duration.

EXAMPLE 3.23. Mozart, Symphony No. 40 in G Minor, K. 550, I, mm. 21–28.

Additive, cumulative, and countercumulative durational patterns occur on various structural levels, from the level of the motive to that of a phrase to that of a period, and so on. For instance, in Example 3.23 three different structural levels are analyzed from Mozart's Symphony No. 40. A bracket marks the beginning and end of each closed durational pattern, which is determined without reference to other parameters. So, for instance, on the lowest structural level the durations in the first measure of Example 3.23 are organized into the cumulative durational pattern ♫ ♩. The first two eighth notes are additive, but their motion is arrested by the cumulative quarter note or quarter note plus quarter rest that follow. The same type of *aab* (anapestic) grouping is found on the next higher structural level in measures 21–22: the additive patterns ♫♩,♫♩ are followed by the longer, cumulative durational pattern ♫♩♩ ♪ . The rest that follows the second quarter note makes it seem longer than the first. This same durational patterning is repeated in measures 23–24, 25–26, and essentially in 27–28 where the whole note (which is a point of elision) is the longest duration in the series and accordingly marks the point of greatest repose.[48] Therefore, on the highest structural level shown in Example 3.23, measures 21–26 create an additive pattern (*aaa*) which is closed by the cumulative durational pattern in measures 27–28 (thus: *aaab*).

With regard to simple and compound duration, then, additive and counter-cumulative patterns are generally intensifying, though they may lead to a concluding, cumulative duration. Cumulative durational patterns create durational closure. Cumulative patterns that conform to previous patterns can produce strong closure because the repeated pattern implies a specific point of conclusion for the series of cumulative durations. Ordinarily, processes and patterns in other parameters help the listener judge which cumulative duration will conclude a pattern, since a series of cumulative durations *per se* does not imply a specific point of conclusion. Durational patterns can help create or enhance closure on various structural levels.

SIMPLE AND COMPOUND TIMBRE

Simple and compound timbre are secondary parameters that define the tone quality, or tone color, of simple and compound elements, respectively. Timbre may be defined as "that characteristic of a tone which depends on its harmonic structure as modified by absolute pitch and total intensity. The harmonic structure is expressed in terms of the number, distribution, and relative intensity of its partials."[49]

Whereas harmonies can be ordered according to their degree of concordance, pitches according to their specific register, dynamics according to their loudness, and durations according to their length, it is unclear how timbres might be ordered along a single dimension.[50] Recent studies have suggested that our perception of timbre has two essential dimensions, one defined by the spectral distribution of energy in the sonority and one defined by the transient characteristics of the sonority.[51] Thus, multidimensional scaling has produced the basis for a model in which specific timbres can be represented as points in a timbral space.

Somehow the mind perceives processes and patterns in harmonies, pitches, dynamics, and durations rather easily, but not in timbres. Now it is true that we readily recognize timbral differences between sounds, but generally speaking in tonal music and in much nontonal music we do not perceive timbral processes or specific timbral relationships between sounds—at least not between timbres produced by different instruments.[52] As Stockhausen has said: "we only hear that one instrument is different than another, but not that they stand in specific relationship to one another."[53] As a result of training, as well as perceived similarities in transients, we tend to categorize sounds according to their general classification (string, woodwind, brass, percussion) or particular classification (such as violin, oboe, cornet, timpani) based on what means were used to produce the sound. Thus, for instance, we are likely to regard the passage in Example 3.24 as an alternation of strings and woodwinds rather than an alternation of two unique timbres *per se*. That is, with respect to tone color we frequently think of sounds in terms of how they were produced rather than paying strict attention to the actual timbres of sounds (in tonal music, at least). In

EXAMPLE 3.24. Tchaikovsky, Symphony No. 6 in B Minor, op. 74, III, mm. 226–27.

fact one gets the impression that for some writers timbre identification and instrument identification amount to the same thing.[54]

Perhaps the primary reason we tend to identify timbre with particular instruments or voices is the fact that in much of Western music timbre has been used to differentiate parts of the musical texture rather than create hierarchical structures. Indeed, it is impossible to build such structures without defining timbral closure, and since timbres cannot be ordered along a single dimension and there is no kind of timbral "tonic" to which other timbres are related, there is little we can say about closure. It seems clear that certain timbres are associated with tension and are often perceived as intensifying, such as the tone colors of cornets and trumpets. In contrast, the tone colors of flutes and violins seem generally less tensive. Moreover, we can say that, because pure tones are devoid of upper partials which can otherwise cause beats and produce roughness, duller timbres enhance concordance and closure. So, for example, a specific triad played by three flutes is somewhat more concordant than the same triad played by three oboes, since the flute's tone quality is rather pure but the oboe's quite rich throughout their respective registral and dynamic ranges.[55] Also, through repetition a particular timbre (or kind of timbre) may be established as the norm, as a string timbre is the norm in symphonies of the classical period, and a return to the norm may be a necessary, but insufficient, condition for closure on high structural levels.

In general, simple and compound timbre are important for articulating events because an abrupt change in timbre is often an indication that something new has begun. However, simple and compound timbre are not important for creating and enhancing closure in tonal music of the eighteenth and nineteenth centuries, and in general it is unclear how timbre might be used to produce closure in works from other time periods.[56]

COMPONENTS

The final secondary parameter to consider is that of components, or the number of identifiable and differentiated strata in the musical fabric. It is by virtue of components that we can differentiate simple and compound parameters. Note that components refers to the *number* of concurrent lines, not to texture, which refers to the way in which listeners organize the lines into a ground, a figure or figures with a ground, or concurrent figures. Furthermore, the number of components is independent of the number of vocal or orchestral parts. For instance, there may be more than one component in one-part (monophonic) music such as a fugue in one of J. S. Bach's sonatas for solo violin.[57] In addition, one can add parts to a particular passage without increasing the number of components as long as the new parts duplicate individual strata already in the music. In measures 341–43 of the second movement of Sibelius's Symphony No. 4 (Example 3.26), the oboe and clarinet parts double the violin part at the unison, so the three orchestral parts constitute only one component in the fabric. In contrast, both the viola and violin lines are components even though the viola doubles the violin at the octave, because the octave is a differentiated strata in the fabric.

In the last few measures of this movement, the number of components shrinks from eight to one (Example 3.25; compare Example 3.26). In measure 345 there are

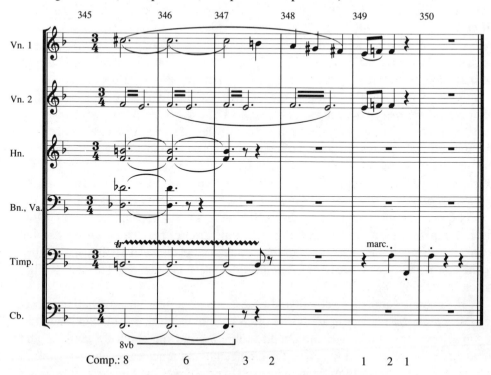

EXAMPLE 3.25. Sibelius, Symphony No. 4 in A Minor, op. 63, II, mm. 345–50.

eight components: bass, timpani, viola (doubled by cello), bassoon (doubled by clarinet, oboe, and flute 2), horn 2 and 4, horn 1 and 3, violin 2, and violin 1. The bassoons, clarinets, oboes, and flute 2 all sustain the same D♭4, though not for the same duration; nevertheless, the four instrumental parts together define one component. Likewise the violas and cellos sustain the same pitch and constitute one component. When the bassoons and violas drop out in measure 346 there are only six components remaining. That number is reduced to three in the next measure when the horns and basses drop out. A moment later the timpani stops playing and there are only two components, which reduce to one component when the violins play in unison in measure 349. Momentarily the violins overlap the entrance of the timpani to create two components before the final notes in the timpani.

The parameter of components is closely tied to compound dynamics, since an increase in components generally results in increased compound dynamics, and a decrease in components generally results in decreased compound dynamics. Moreover, a decrease in components typically reduces the complexity of the texture and lessens the number of harmonic and pitch implications in the music. As a result of reduced tension and complexity, then, a process of decreasing components will tend to enhance closure. Such a process can imply a specific point of conclusion: the arrival at a single component. That is illustrated in measures 345–49 of Example 3.26 where, as one might expect, the reduction in components is accompanied by a reduction in textural complexity.

Example 3.26 illustrates another important point: when tonal syntax is attenuated and strong final closure is not created by the primary parameters, several corresponding secondary parameters can create final closure. To be sure, there is tonal melodic closure on F in measure 349, but the traditional means of producing closure, namely a strong cadence, is lacking. Instead, closure is signaled by the descending registral pitch patterns in the oboes, clarinets, bassoons, first violins, violas, and cellos in measures 340–49, as well as by the generally decreasing compound dynamics throughout the passage. The descending registral pitch pattern in the first violins leads to closure in measure 349 on the F, which is implied by the sustained F pedal as well as the E/F tremolo in the second violins. A process of generally increasing concordance in measures 343–48 is followed by *decreasing* concordance in measure 348, leading to a climactic dissonance of E/F/F♯ on the last beat before a reversal to the unison of measure 349. Thus there is concordant closure in measure 349. Cumulative simple and compound durations in the violins at measures 348–49 and the timpani in measures 349–50 (because the last F3 is followed by silence) enhance final closure. And, of course, the reiterated tonic pitches in the timpani (which conform to the conventional closing gesture of Example 2.8) are a means of emphasizing and prolonging the tonic F, which is the goal of this entire abating structure; on the lowest hierarchical level the final F3 is a return to the initial marcato F3, thereby strengthening closure.

*   *   *

EXAMPLE 3.26. Sibelius, Symphony No. 4 in A Minor, op. 63, II, mm. 340–50.

EXAMPLE 3.26 (*cont.*)

Understanding how the individual secondary parameters can enhance and create closure is a significant step toward understanding how we perceive closure in music. What is most important, though, is how the various parameters interact to create closure in music. Though we lack experimental studies that account for our perception of closure as a result of such interaction, there are some general observations that can be made.

Whether because of nature or nurture, we tend to associate particular parametric processes with others that typically produce the same abating or intensifying effect. Thus, as Schoenberg states: "nearly all musicians combine a change in dynamics, consciously or unconsciously, with a change of tempo; a crescendo is usually accompanied by an accelerando, a diminuendo by a rallentando. . . . It is, at least, almost universal practice to make a crescendo in a melody that rises . . . sequences are almost always performed as a 'build-up,' dynamically as well as in tempo."[58]

With respect to abating processes and patterns, it seems clear that we associate a diminuendo not only with a rallentando, but also with descending pitch patterns. Passages that combine these three kinds of abatements are common in Western music; see, for instance, Example 2.4. Moreover, abatements in concordance and components are generally associated with a musical context that more often than not is characterized by an abatement in one or more of the other parameters.

We would expect, then, that abating closure is commonly dependent upon corresponding processes or patterns in more than one secondary parameter. Most often, abatements in durations are crucial to producing closure, because durations are probably the most potent secondary parameter for articulating form. That is so because durations separate things; the longer a particular duration, the more the preceding part is separated from what follows. Components also can be an important organizing force, at least in part because abatements in components are typically accompanied by a substantial reduction in dynamics and often by an overall increase in concordance.

Generally speaking, secondary parameters must be corresponding if they are to make a strong impact on closure, since individually they are weak relative to the primary parameters. Ongoing processes in primary parameters divert the listener's attention from processes and patterns in secondary parameters, which, on the other hand, can be an important organizing force when the primary parameters are static. Therefore, secondary parameters are usually important for shaping the conclusion of a tonic prolongation following cadential closure.

The fact that secondary parameters are frequently corresponding means that a more or less specific point of closure may be implied by the combination of abating processes or patterns. That is, though we are typically unsure when a diminuendo, durational pattern, or concordant process will end, the listener can often anticipate the conclusion based on information provided by the musical context. Accordingly, we may justifiably speak of simple dynamic closure in measure 481 of Example 3.12, even though from the standpoint of dynamics alone we might not be able to predict a specific point of closure.

Composers throughout the eighteenth and nineteenth centuries relied upon cadential closure, typically supported by secondary parameters, to articulate formal structure. When composers began avoiding traditional cadences, they needed to find another way to articulate musical form, and many of them turned to the use of secondary parameters. Since Mahler was one of the most influential composers of the late nineteenth and early twentieth centuries, how he used secondary parameters to create closure should be of particular interest and significance.

CHAPTER 4

Secondary Parameters and
Closure in Mahler

Mahler was a composer of tonal music, but there is general agreement that his works exemplify the gradual breakdown of tonal syntax—especially tonal *harmonic* syntax—during the late nineteenth and early twentieth centuries. Thus, Deryck Cooke observes: "Others have noticed how Mahler's harmonic explorations advanced the disruption of tonality begun in Wagner's *Tristan* towards the early free atonality of Schoenberg,"[1] and Hans Tischler asserts: "He was one of the most outstanding and most influential instigators of the crisis in tonality which reached its climax in the quarter century after his death."[2] In particular, Mahler's late symphonic works, except for the Eighth Symphony,[3] illustrate the weakening of tonal harmony as an organizing force.

The gradual decline of tonal harmonic syntax in Mahler's music is manifested in a variety of ways, especially in the pairing of two tonics in the same work (such as C and E♭ in the Second Symphony), the avoidance of strong traditional cadential progressions, and the frequency of nontonal passages or passages of vague tonality, largely a result of increased chromaticism in a lean polyphonic texture. Analysts generally agree that the breakdown of tonal syntax is most evident in works composed after the Fourth Symphony—that is, after 1900. For instance, according to Donald Mitchell:

> In this period [up to 1900] Mahler was an unambiguously tonal composer, though he often used tonality in a very fresh way. There is certainly no feeling of exhaustion about his language, in part because he was working naturally in a style that was often unabashedly diatonic, with occasional forays into highly chromatic harmony. . . . Only later did his tonality diminish in stability, with a pervasive chromaticism of his harmonic style.

This trend, though, is already apparent in his Fourth Symphony, which for all the diatonic character of some of its materials, sometimes moves into an elaborately chromatic motivic polyphony where tonality becomes exiguous. . . .[4]

The use of what Dika Newlin calls "progressive tonality"[5] or what Robert Bailey refers to as a "double-tonic complex"[6] contributes to increased chromaticism in Mahler's music and helps substantiate the claim that the composer used tonality "in a very fresh way." The mixture of G major and E major in Symphony No. 4, especially the finale, is an oft-cited example. Christopher Orlo Lewis asserts that the majority of Mahler's mature works are predicated on co-existent tonics, usually a third apart, and he cites various means by which the double-tonic complex is disclosed: "1. Juxtaposition of musical fragments implying the two tonics in succession or alternation, 2. Mixture of the two tonalities, exploiting ambiguous and common harmonic functions, 3. Use of a tonic sonority created by conflation of the two tonic triads, 4. Superposition of lines or texture in one key upon those in another, and 5. Some combination of the above."[7] All of these procedures helped weaken tonal harmonic syntax, and furthermore the use of co-existent tonics effectively reduces the structural role of the dominant as a contrasting tonal center in many Mahler works. Even so, other contributing factors probably had more impact on the relative importance of secondary parameters for creating musical structures.

The most important factor is simply the avoidance of traditional authentic cadences, especially in Symphonies 5, 6, 7, and 9, in *Das Lied von der Erde,* and in most songs written after 1900. In many of these works authentic cadences are infrequent, and in fact traditional authentic cadences in the tonic can be quite rare, as they are for instance in *Nun seh' ich wohl, warum so dunkle Flammen, Um Mitternacht,* and *Ich bin der Welt abhanden gekommen;* as well as in Symphony No. 2, III; No. 3, I and III; No. 5, I and II; No. 6, I and III (the Scherzo);[8] No. 7, I; No. 9, III; and No. 10, I.[9] Thus with respect to the symphonies, traditional authentic cadences are generally least common in the first movements and fast or moderately fast inner movements of Symphonies 5, 6, 7, and 9, as well as the first movement of 10.

The lack of strong traditional cadential progressions in much of Mahler's mature music is of fundamental significance for this study, because such progressions are the most common means of creating substantial syntactic closure in tonal music.

At times Mahler simply avoids clear cadences, while at other times he creatively adapts the traditional cadential formulas to his own purposes. For instance, in a few movements such as the third movements of the Second and Ninth Symphonies, Mahler establishes some sort of $\flat$II harmony—rather than the dominant—as the penultimate chord in a closing harmonic progression. Example 4.1 gives the closing measures from the third movement of Symphony No. 9, in which $\flat$II$^{6\sharp}$ (which contains the same tritone as the dominant) is a substitute for the dominant.[10] The $\flat$II$^{6\sharp}$ as well as the $\flat$II triad often substitute for the dominant in Symphony No. 2, III.

Even in songs or movements of works where traditional cadential progressions

EXAMPLE 4.1. Mahler, Symphony No. 9, III, mm. 665–67.

are fairly common, syntactic closure is sometimes less than decisive because the cadences lack strength. In such cases Mahler frequently weakens the fundamental dominant-to-tonic progression by reducing the tension of the dominant chord. Several times in the second (*Andante*) movement of the Sixth Symphony, for example, the penultimate dominant harmony in a cadential progression lacks a third or a seventh.[11] In the opening movement of Symphony No. 3, complete dominant seventh chords in root position are relatively rare; Mahler is more likely to use dominant triads (occasionally augmented) or dominant seventh chords without the third.

Mahler also weakens the impact of traditional cadential progressions in another way. At times, especially in the later symphonies, abating secondary parameters reduce the tensive effect of a dominant harmony, and the tonic that follows is marked by an abrupt change in orchestration or perhaps dynamics (or both). As a result, the tonic sounds very much like the *beginning* of a phrase and rather little like the conclusion of the preceding phrase. The $V_{(7)}$–I progression is greatly weakened because the dominant harmony seems separated, in a sense, from the tonic.[12] In some instances the separation is explicit: in the third movement of the Fifth Symphony

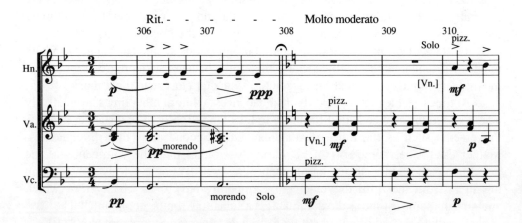

EXAMPLE 4.2. Mahler, Symphony No. 5, III, mm. 306–10.

(Example 4.2), measures 306–7 follow a passage (measures 277–305) characterized by alternating phrases between a *corno obligato* on the one hand, and various wind and string instruments on the other. The short phrases (measures 271–81, 282–85, 286–89, 290–92, 293–96, 297–300, 301–5) all end with a fermata, and except at measure 305 the ends of phrases in the horn are marked with a diminuendo and the instruction *verklingend*. Thus, the listener may rightly anticipate that the horn phrase beginning at the end of measure 305 will close when the diminuendo in measure 307 reaches the point of silence. The tonic in measure 308 begins a new passage.

Another procedure that limits the influence of the primary parameters in articulating closure is Mahler's frequent use of two- or three-part contrapuntal fabrics in which traditional cadential progressions are weakly implied or entirely absent. Perhaps partly as a consequence of the relative absence of strong traditional cadences, in many works Mahler anchors long passages to a particular tonal center by employing one or more pedal points, which provide tonal stability but also restrict the use of traditional harmonic progressions.[13] The result can be that in such passages processes in secondary parameters become more important for shaping musical form, as we will see in the introduction to Symphony No. 1. In later works Mahler used pedal points less often, and tonal syntax was further weakened.

> The fundamental principle in Mahler's technique of composition was two-part counterpoint. This was a natural means for his expression of what lies at the root of all his work: conflict. Conflict is not satisfactorily conveyed by melody cushioned by changing harmonies. For Mahler the essence of his style seems to have been associated with the use of bare intervals, fourths and fifths, and pedal-points. As he developed, and as his scoring became ever more sinewy, he abandoned pedal-points so that his two-part contrapuntal form became detached from the conventional sense of tonality, with each part independent of the other and liable to separate development, as in the Ninth Symphony. [See Example 4.3.][14]

EXAMPLE 4.3. Mahler, Symphony No. 9, IV, mm. 28–32.

The weakening of tonal closure in the music of Mahler and his contemporaries had a profound influence on twentieth-century composers, who explored new ways to create and articulate musical structures. It is instructive to study the inventive ways in which Mahler himself compensated for the weakening of tonal syntax by relying on processes and patterns in secondary parameters. In this chapter we will look in detail at his use of secondary parameters to articulate musical structures, especially using processes of dissolution. Following a careful analysis of the introduction and exposition of the first movement in Symphony No. 1, we will consider selected musical examples from Mahler's oeuvre that illustrate the varied strategies he employed to create closure. Since our primary concern is with Mahler's use of abating closure instead of cadential closure, we will examine larger-scale closure, from that of the phrase to that of an entire movement or work.

Three different kinds of passages will be discussed: (1) those where abatements in secondary parameters are terminally synchronized with cadential closure, (2) those where cadential closure is followed by a prolonged tonic whose close is created by abating secondary parameters, and (3) those where abatements in secondary parameters themselves are primarily responsible for defining closure. Presumably passages of the third type will be more frequent in those movements of the mature works where tonality is not as strong an organizing force.

In the musical examples, abatements and intensifications will continue to be indicated by A⤳ and V^7 respectively. As observed earlier, abatements and intensifications are observable *trends* in music. For instance, with regard to registral pitch,

is an abatement. Essentially motionless or undirected successions of elements (such as repeated or alternating pitches) are connected by a dashed horizontal arrow ---→. The arrival of closure is indicated by a vertical slash |, and the state of relative repose following closure is designated by a solid horizontal line. For instance, with respect to registral pitch:

A solid horizontal line designates the relative repose that follows the end of an abatement, even if there is no closure.

In the diagrams secondary parameters will be denoted by four-letter abbreviations:

RPit = Registral Pitch	SDur = Simple Duration
Conc = Concordance	CDur = Compound Duration
SDyn = Simple Dynamics	STim = Simple Timbre
CDyn = Compound Dynamics	CTim = Compound Timbre
Comp = Components	

Where there is more than one prominent instrumental or vocal line in a particular passage, the diagram will indicate which line is the basis for the analysis of the simple parameters. In Example 4.6, for instance, perhaps the most important figure in measures 55–58 is the cello line, but the descending fourths in the English horn, flute, and then the clarinet are also an important figure—which becomes especially significant when the cellos drop out. One could analyze both figures for all the simple parameters, but to avoid complicating the diagram it is more helpful to decide which figure is most prominent with respect to a particular simple parameter. Accordingly, the pattern of descending fourths in the woodwinds is analyzed for simple durations (SDur)[15]; the cello and then the clarinet lines are the basis for the analysis of registral pitch (RPit); and the cello, flute, and clarinet lines are analyzed for simply dynamics (SDyn). Since durational patterns occur on various structural levels, there will usually be several different durational processes that can be included in the diagram of a musical example. In most cases the one or two lowest structural levels will be indicated, though the very lowest level may be omitted so that the diagrams may be more easily read. For instance, in Example 4.6 the diagram of the simple durational pattern omits the lowest level of organization, which is a two-note motive of a quarter note followed by a quarter note tied over to a dotted quarter note ♩ ♩⌣♩.; the longer tied duration creates closure on the lowest level. The tied durations, which become ever longer, are the basis for the next higher level, which is shown in the diagram. The analysis of compound durations in Example 4.6 shows the lowest two levels only in the first two measures; throughout the example, the compound durations that result from the eighth-note triplets in the cellos and the eighth notes in the clarinet all lead to closure in measure 58 on the quarter note (on the second beat) that is at the same time part of an ongoing series of quarter-note compound durations which closes with the half-note compound duration in measure 59. High-level patterns of particular importance will be diagrammed or else mentioned in the text.

The musical examples from *Kindertotenlieder* and Symphonies 5, 6, and 7 are all based upon the critical editions of Mahler's works by the Internationale Gustav Mahler Gesellschaft.[16] Owing to difficulties in reaching agreement with the publisher of the other Mahler works cited, examples from these works are based on editions now in the public domain, and therefore may occasionally differ slightly from the current critical editions. None of the differences are significant. All parts are at their actual sounding pitch. Most examples are orchestral reductions.[17] Readers should consult the appropriate score for the complete musical text, which is the basis for the diagrams. The appendix gives measure numbers for all the rehearsal numbers in the symphonies.

*   *   *

The introduction (measures 1–62) to the opening movement of the First Symphony consists of a dominant pedal (usually heard in several registers) over which bird calls, fanfares, and various short phrases are heard; the first forty measures are given in Example 4.4. The sustained dominant pedal (on A) suggests that musical

EXAMPLE 4.4. Mahler, Symphony No. 1, I, mm. 1–40.

EXAMPLE 4.4 (*cont.*)

EXAMPLE 4.4 (*cont.*)

EXAMPLE 4.4 (cont.)

EXAMPLE 4.4 (*cont.*)

EXAMPLE 4.4 (*cont.*)

EXAMPLE 4.4 (*cont.*)

EXAMPLE 4.4 (*cont.*)

structure is generally articulated by secondary parameters. This is the case. The descending fourth A–E, a motive first introduced in three different octaves in the woodwinds at measure 3, initiates a descending phrase in the oboe

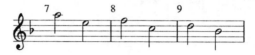

which is doubled by the bassoons. When the descent reaches D in measure 9, the listener anticipates closure with the arrival at A4, not only because it would continue the pattern of descending perfect fourths, but also because A4 is an octave below the initial pitch of the pattern and is concordant with the dominant pedal—indeed, A4 is one of the pedal tones. Thus, the pattern implies registral pitch closure and concordant closure on A4. Closure is delayed by the B♭, which is discordant with the dominant pedal and heightens the expectation of a resolution to A. After clarinet fanfares prolong the discordant B♭ harmony in measures 9–13, the flute and bassoons surprisingly ascend to B, thereby implying a continued ascent to C or C♯, either of which would be concordant with the dominant pedal. The quickly fading flute and bassoon lines (marked *morendo* at measure 14) suggest that the arrival at C in measure 15 is a temporary point of closure.

When the pattern of descending fourths from measure 7 is repeated in the woodwinds beginning at measure 18, the B♭ resolves directly to the anticipated A, which is a whole note in duration. Consequently, closure on the A in measure 21 is created by processes and patterns in registral pitch, durations, and concordance. We still have not heard the implied direct descent from D to A, however.

Durational closure ends the trumpet fanfares that begin in measure 22. The main fanfare statement in the first two trumpets reaches closure with the quarter note tied to the half note in measures 25–26; the echo in the third trumpet (*in der Ferne*) likewise closes with a three-beat duration in measures 26–27. The simple durational closure in the third trumpet is supported by compound durational closure at the end of measure 26: the reiterated descending fourths played by the woodwinds in an eighth-note compound durational pattern in measures 25–27 close with the two-beat duration in the bass clarinet at the end of measure 26 and beginning of measure 27 (Example 4.5).

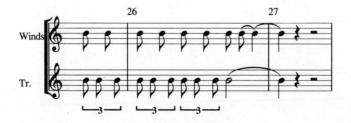

EXAMPLE 4.5. Mahler, Symphony No. 1, I, mm. 26–27: durational patterns.

Finally in measures 28–31 the repeated pattern of descending fourths in the strings fulfills the implication of a direct descent from D to A, which occurs in measures 30–31 to close the phrase. The direct descent from D to A is foreshadowed in the cuckoo call of the clarinet in measure 30. In the measures that follow, simple durational closure marks the ends of phrases in the horns (measures 32–36) and trumpets (measures 36–37), and the series of descending octaves in the woodwinds (measures 37–38). The trumpet and woodwind parts of measures 36–38 are similar to measures 25–27, and compound durational closure in measure 38 is conformant with the compound durational closure at the end of measure 26.

The succession of phrases after measure 28, unlike that in measures 1–27, is made more continuous by the overlapping entrances of the various instrumental phrases: the clarinet provides ongoing motion from measure 30 into measure 32, the trumpets enter in measure 36 before the horn passage is entirely over, and the chord progression in the flutes and oboes in measures 37–40 helps to connect the end of the passage in measure 38 to the repeat of the horn phrase at measure 40. Mahler continues this procedure of overlapping phrases in measures 40 to 47, whereupon a new, mostly chromatic ascending line is heard in the cellos and basses. A degree of tension is created by the ascent of this line almost two octaves to G in measure 55, and the intensification is bolstered by the diminution of the descending fourth pattern in the horns at measure 51 and the stretto entrances of the same pattern in the horns and the clarinet in measures 52–55.

At measure 55, however, the intensifying process is reversed and abating processes in several secondary parameters from measure 55 to measure 62 bring the introduction to a close. The processes are diagrammed in Example 4.6. Registral pitch closure occurs in the cellos in measure 58 because of the descending, conjunct return to A2, the initial pitch of the pattern that began in measure 47. The cello line fades to silence to create simple dynamic closure at the beginning of measure 59. At the same time the absence of any attack on the downbeat of measure 59 brings about compound durational closure. Other abating processes in simple durations, concordance, dynamics, and components contribute to the impression in measures 59–62 that the introduction is drawing to a close—that it is in some sense dissolving away. The abatements are not terminally synchronized in any two parameters so there is no single point of strong closure, which is not surprising since this is only the end of the introduction. However, the combined effect of the simultaneous abatements—most notably in dynamics and components in measures 55–59—is considerable, especially following directly after the intensification in measures 47–55.

The overall effect is one of *dissolution* created primarily by thinning texture and fading compound dynamics, a common process in Mahler's music. Prominent closure is created in measure 61 by the ultimate reduction to a single component—indeed, a single instrument—which is striking because it marks the end of the dominant pedal as well as the close of an abatement with respect to components. All that remains is a restatement of the opening figure from measure 3, now heard in diminution and at a different pitch in order to prepare the main theme of the exposition.

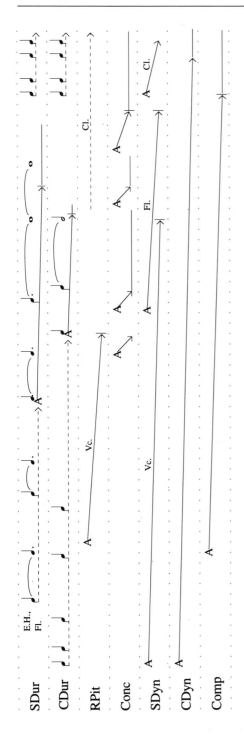

EXAMPLE 4.6. Mahler, Symphony No. 1, I, mm. 55–62.

Processes in secondary parameters, so important for articulating musical form in the introduction, are also crucial in shaping musical form in the exposition, where no strong syntactic closure occurs until the perfect full cadence in the dominant in measures 129–35. The end of the primary theme in the cellos (measures 63–74) is indicated by the arrival at simple durational closure in measure 71, at which point the cellos continue to sustain their final pitch while the now familiar cuckoo call in the clarinet provides a sense of ongoing motion leading to a restatement of the theme beginning with the anacruses to measure 75. The end of the restatement is shaped by diminishing dynamics, a reduction in components, and a generally descending pitch pattern in the violins and violas in measures 81–83, though the phrase does not reach closure. Instead the running eighth-note pattern in the violas leads directly to a new passage beginning in measure 84. As in measures 81–83, decreasing compound dynamics and a descending melodic line in the violins at measures 106–8 and 115–16 help articulate the next two passages.

After the perfect full cadence in the dominant at measures 129–35, Mahler prolongs the A-major triad in a traditional way: dominant seventh and tonic chords alternate over a tonic pedal until a final, extended tonic is reached (measure 152). Since the primary parameters are essentially static, it is not surprising that secondary parameters are used to shape the tonic prolongation. Registral pitch and dynamics are especially important in giving shape to the tonic prolongation, as is shown in Example 4.7. The music builds to the climactic fortissimo of measures 151–152, and then the passage seems to subside. An overall abatement in registral pitch and dynamics leads to greater repose at measure 155, in which there is simple durational closure in the strings (top staff). Measure 155 is heard as a point of arrival in part because in measures 135–62 the primary parameters define consecutive four-measure phrases, which results in a large-scale rhythmic structure with emphasis on the beginning of each phrase, including the beginning of measure 155. The next four-measure phrase begins at measure 159, where concordant closure is achieved and abatements in registral pitch (in the horns, bottom staff) and compound dynamics come to an end.[18] At the same time the first violins ascend an octave as part of a rising line back to an A6 harmonic, with which they began the movement. The return to an A6 harmonic and octave A recalls the introduction, of course, and with the addition of the descending octaves in the clarinet, horn, and bassoon the listener will recognize a conformant relationship between measures 159–62 and measures 59–62, which directly preceded the exposition. Therefore, at the same time that the pedal tones and the pattern of descending octaves in measures 159–62 shape the end of the tonic prolongation following closure in measure 159, they also provide a transition back to a repeat of the exposition, or—the second time around—on to the development section.[19]

One of the advantages of using abating closure, then, is that such passages tend to allow for a transition to the next section at the same time that a sense of repose is created or maintained. The dissolution of energy in measures 152–62 creates the opportunity for closure as well as a transition to a section characterized by a thinner texture, softer dynamics, and longer durational values. A dissolution can have the effect of "wiping the slate clean" as Schoenberg noted:

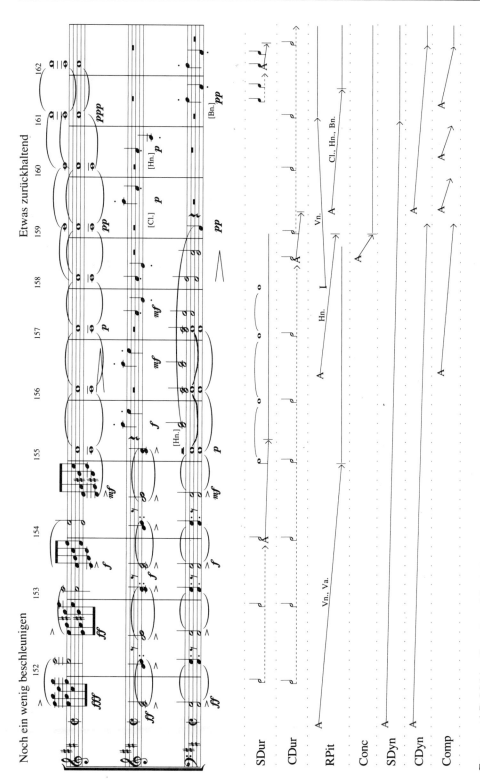

EXAMPLE 4.7. Mahler, Symphony No. 1, I, mm. 152–62.

Dissolution [Auflösung] is the exact counterpart of establishment [Aufstellung], firm formation, shaping. If in these the main objective is, through variation of the basic shapes [Gestalten], to bring out their characteristics as sharply as possible, to interconnect the single Gestalten as closely as possible, to keep the tension among the tones high, the most important thing in dissolution is to drop all characteristics as fast as possible, to let the tensions run off and to liquidate [liquidieren] the obligations of the former Gestalten in such as away that there will be, so to speak, a 'clean slate,' so that the possibility for the appearance of other materials is given.[20]

In Mahler's music a dissolution is not usually accomplished "as fast as possible," though there are examples that seem to fall away rapidly, even to "collapse."[21] We will return to the subject of dissolutions below.

Another significant result of using secondary parameters to shape musical form is the ability to write very continuous music that nevertheless clearly articulates formal structures without necessarily employing strong points of closure. That is, abating processes tend toward repose, and even if an overall abatement is interrupted before reaching closure, the last part of the abatement is a relative point of repose. When the listener recognizes an overall abatement he or she is prepared not only for the conclusion of the particular passage in question, but also for the imminent beginning of another section. Sometimes the overall abatement leads to abating closure, and many times it does not, but in all cases the formal divisions are more or less clear. For instance, in measures 76–80 of Example 4.8 there is a clear abating trend in registral pitch, dynamics, durations, and components, yet there is no strong point of closure. The overall abatement nevertheless convinces the listener that the passage is ending, and the listener anticipates the beginning of another section—in this case, the return at measure 81 of a theme and texture first heard at measure 28.

Thus, an abatement lends itself to situations in which a composer wants to connect different passages without coming to rest: secondary parameters *shape* the end of a passage without reaching closure, and a new passage indicates that the previous section or phrase is over. One can distinguish, then, between shaping the end of a passage—*suggesting* imminent closure—and actually creating abating closure.[22]

The increased use of secondary parameters to shape musical form in Mahler's mature works may be seen as a result of a general trend toward greater continuity, a trend also manifest in fewer strong cadences, more overlapping of phrases and sections, and clearer articulations of beginnings rather than of ends. Natalie Bauer-Lechner's report of comments by Mahler about Karl Löwe reveal Mahler's preoccupation with continuous musical development.

He settled for the piano, whereas a large-scale composition that plumbs the depths of the subject, unconditionally demands the orchestra. Nor can he quite free himself from the old style; he repeats individual stanzas, whereas I have come to recognize a perpetual evolution of the song's content—in other words, through-composition [das Durchkomponieren]—as the true principle of music. In my writing, from the very first, you won't find any more repetition from strophe to strophe; for music is governed by the law of eternal evolution, eternal development—just as the world, even in one and the same spot, is always changing, eternally fresh and new. But of course this development must be progressive, or I don't give a damn for it.[23]

Mahler's interest in continuous music is readily apparent, as the analysis of the opening of Symphony No. 1 indicates. Often in his music the first instance of a

EXAMPLE 4.8. Mahler, Symphony No. 10, I, mm. 76–81.

particular passage has the strongest closure, and repeated conformant passages tend to have weaker closure because there is a greater sense of ongoing motion, whether because of overlapping, elision, or some variation of the passage itself. Compare, for instance, the ends of phrases in measures 1–27 of the introduction to Symphony No. 1, I, with the ends of phrases in measures 28–47. There is more ongoing motion in the latter section. Note, too, the closure at the end of the first phrase of the exposition (measures 63–74) and the lack of clear closure in the conformant passage that immediately follows it. The lack of any strong overall closure—closure on a higher hierarchic level than the phrase—at the ends of many of these phrases is not a weakness. Rather it is indicative of the fact that much of the music of the introduction and exposition is quite continuous, with relatively few clear points of overall closure. Nevertheless, in all these passages the formal articulations on the level of the phrase are fairly clear, primarily because abating processes in secondary parameters make them so, and because the listener can discern phrase structure even when there are elisions or overlappings. That is, probably based in large part on differences in timbre, listeners can distinguish a phrase ending in certain components from a concomitant phrase beginning in other components.

*   *   *

Our analysis of the opening of the first movement of Symphony No. 1 has illustrated some of the strategies that Mahler employed to shape the ends of passages, as well as to create abating closure that defines the conclusion of a passage. In the rest of this chapter we will concentrate attention on examples of abating closure rather than on shaping. Our primary focus will be on examples of closure produced by several corresponding secondary parameters, one or more of which implies and reaches a specific point of repose. The reader will recall from the examples in chapter 3 that abating closure is produced in many different ways; consequently it is difficult to identify standard procedures that Mahler employed in creating such closure. We can, however, draw several general conclusions about how he used secondary parameters to create closure.

Many times a process in only one or two secondary parameters leads to closure, which is supported by abatements in other secondary parameters. It will come as no surprise that processes in simple and compound duration in Mahler's music create closure far more frequently than processes in any of the other secondary parameters. Durations are a potent organizing force because they separate things; the longer a particular duration, the more the preceding part is separated from what follows. In Mahler's music durational abatements are often created by slowing tempo, especially where there is a more or less constant unit of compound durations. Durational closure commonly occurs on all structural levels and in all symphonies. Such closure readily segments the music into motives, phrases, periods, and so forth. Durational closure often occurs apart from any overall abatement in secondary parameters, and is frequently found at points of cadential closure—especially at the ends of movements. In this study, however, our interest in durational closure is with those instances in which an overall abatement defined by secondary parameters, including durations, leads to durational closure. More often than not, such closure occurs on the level of a phrase or on some higher level.

At times abatements in the parameter of components lead to closure, which is supported by abatements (but not necessarily closure) in other secondary parameters. Component closure is forceful not only because we are aware of the tremendous instrumental and vocal resources generally employed by Mahler, but also because a reduction in components is typically accompanied by a substantial reduction in dynamics and often by an overall increase in concordance. The closing of the introduction to the first movement of Symphony No. 1 (Example 4.6) illustrates this point.

Closure in registral pitch or dynamics, as opposed to durations and components, is almost always supported by closure in another secondary parameter (especially duration), and, except in the first two symphonies, the same can be said for closure in concordance. This suggests that for Mahler the parameters of duration and, to a lesser extent, components were the most effective secondary parameters for creating closure. Accordingly, closure is generally enhanced—that is, supported—by abatements in dynamics, registral pitch, and concordance.

In particular, diminishing dynamics and descending registral pitch are often used by Mahler to create closure after a dynamic climax, as illustrated in Example 4.7. After a fortissimo climax in measures 151–52 (with triple fortissimo markings in the violins and viola) the music subsides to pianissimo octave As in measure 159. Closure in one or more secondary parameters, most often duration or components (not dynamics), typically concludes an abating passage such as this. The pedal in the basses is also typical, though a pedal is less likely in the later symphonies with the exception of No. 8. Examples of an abatement following a dynamic climax are common in Mahler's music, and they create the overall effect of dissolution.

DISSOLUTION

Dissolution may be defined as a process whereby some musical passage, motive, or chord dissolves in some sense, either falling or fading away (or both). Generally a dissolution is abating, as illustrated in Example 4.6 where the music of measures 55–56 is dissolved to the solo clarinet motive of measures 61–62, and in Example 4.7 where the prolonged A-major chord is reduced to octave As. Both examples are characterized by descending figures,[24] diminishing dynamics, and thinning texture, all of which generally characterize abating dissolutions in Mahler's works. Durational and concordant closure, often found in dissolutions, are also common to both examples.

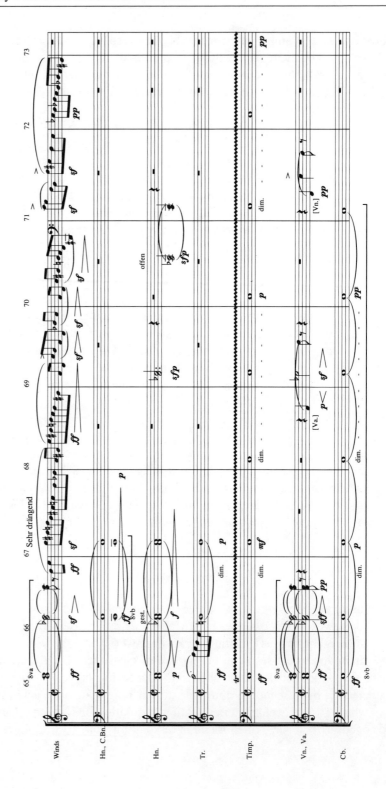

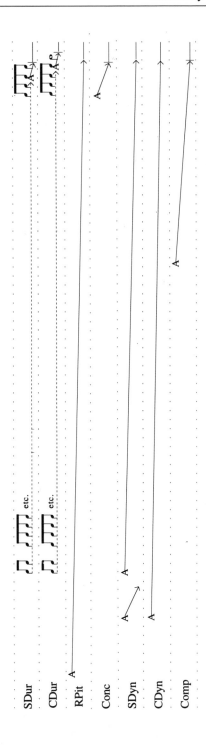

EXAMPLE 4.9. Mahler, Symphony No. 5, II, mm. 65–73.

It is difficult to generalize about types of dissolutions, but for the sake of discussion one can distinguish three kinds according to their characteristic effect:

1) *collapse:* the music seems to crumble and fall away rapidly
2) *fragmentation:* the music seems to dissipate, to separate into parts and vanish
3) *subsidence:* the music seems to "melt away" or fade, losing force gradually.[25]

Of these by far the most common are instances of subsidence, including Examples 4.6 and 4.7. We will examine many other examples of subsidence later in the chapter, but first let us consider the other types of dissolution, beginning with gestures of collapse.

COLLAPSE

Generally speaking, a collapse is a dissolution in which one or more quick descending figures, often a chromatic scale or even a portamento, are accompanied by a relatively sudden decrease in components and dynamics. A collapse often follows some kind of dynamic climax, and characteristically serves to effect a transition from one section to another. A typical example is found in the second movement of the Fifth Symphony. The first major section in the movement builds toward a fortissimo climax on a i_4^6 chord in measure 59, after which descending lines in the winds and strings (measures 59–61) ease tension somewhat. The horns and trumpets drop out in measure 61, but in the same measure—marked *Drängend* ("pressing") in the score—the upper strings and trombones begin another ascent that builds to a fortissimo climax in measures 65–66 (Example 4.9) quite like that of measures 58–59 except that this time the A6 pitch in the flutes and violins is supported by a second inversion F-major chord rather than the tonic A minor. In measures 66–73 descending pitch patterns in the woodwinds, diminishing dynamics, and decreasing components rapidly reduce tension, and the whole structure seems to collapse like a house of cards to the C pedal in the timpani.[26] The abatements in registral pitch, dynamics, and components are terminally synchronized with durational closure in measure 73, which concludes the first large section (A) of the movement.[27]

Note that the C pedal in the timpani, as well as the inverted F-minor chord in measure 66, prepares the next section, which is in F minor. Thus Mahler used the dissolution shown in Example 4.9 not only to close the opening A section of the movement, but also to bring about a transition to the B section that follows. The C pedal is resolved to F in measure 79, where a new march theme begins.

A gesture of collapse in *Des Antonius von Padua Fischpredigt* also serves both as a conclusion and as a means of making a transition to the next section.[28] This time, however, there is no pedal tone and the dissolution leads directly to a new key. The song is in C minor and consists of five strophes, the first three of which end with the refrain "Kein Predigt niemalen den Fischen [Stockfisch', Krebsen] so g'fallen." The end of the first strophe in measures 47–48 is marked by a ♭II⁶♯–I cadence in C, which is followed by a clarinet melody that leads into a descending succession of harmonies IV–III–♭II–i. The end of the second strophe is marked by the same ♭II⁶♯–I cadence, and again the clarinet begins its refrain. This time, though, the clarinet melody leads into a gesture of collapse in measures 94–99 (Example 4.10). Descending registral

Example 4.10. Mahler, *Des Antonius von Padua Fischpredigt,* mm. 94–99.

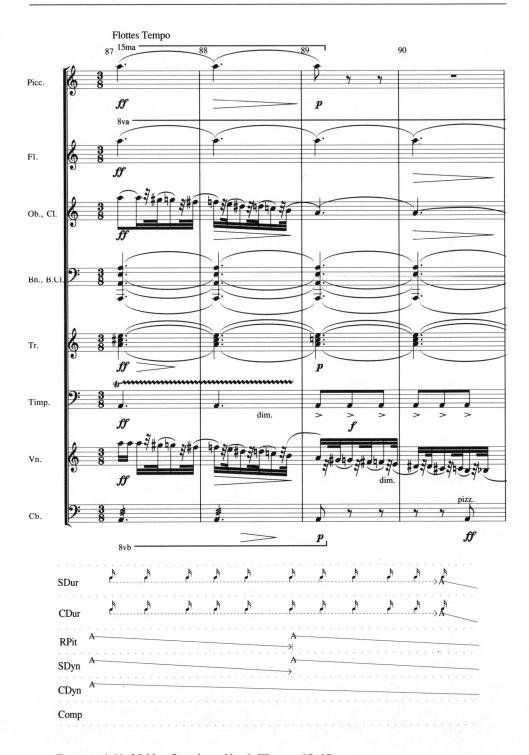

EXAMPLE 4.11. Mahler, Symphony No. 6, III, mm. 87–97.

EXAMPLE 4.11 (*cont.*)

pitch and decreasing dynamics shape the collapse, which reaches concordant and component closure in measure 99. Note how the pattern of descending thirds changes subtly at the end of measure 98, where the viola and cello lines move in contrary motion, to converge on F on the downbeat of the next measure. The third strophe is set in F major, and it is followed by an abbreviated strophe that moves to G major. When the clarinet refrain returns (at measure 149), it leads to another collapse like that in Example 4.10, but this time the harmonic transition is from G major to C minor (measure 159).

As observed earlier, a dissolution can have the effect of "wiping the slate clean," and that effect is clearly exemplified by the collapse in measures 87–91 of Symphony No. 6, III (Example 4.11). The third movement is a scherzo and trio, and there are very few points of substantial cadential closure—none at all in the tonic. Therefore, abating processes in secondary parameters are particularly important in defining closure at the ends of phrases and sections. The collapse shown in Example 4.11 concludes the first scherzo section of the movement. It follows a closing passage of alternating $\flat II_6$–I(i) harmonies (measures 82–87) that ends on the tonic major.[29] The descending chromatic scale patterns and decreasing dynamics in measures 87–91 prepare the listener for the registral pitch and durational closure in measure 91. Measures 87–91 extend the tonic harmony and bring the section to a close.

In this particular instance the collapsing musical structure has a stable and solid foundation, the root of the prolonged tonic, and strong closure occurs in measure 91 when the chord is dissolved to its essence in what amounts to a kind of musical "meltdown." The extended A3/A2 octave in the second violins and bass clarinet is overlapped by the beginning of a transition that leads to the first trio section (measures 98–198). Having concluded the scherzo, Mahler builds a bridge to the trio.

The bridge in measures 91–97 is shaped primarily by an increase and subsequent decrease in components. Diminishing dynamics, increasing durations (owing to the slowing tempo), and decreasing components contribute to the sense of dissolution in measures 96–97. As in many of his transitions, Mahler reduces the music to one pivotal note—the common note between the tonic of the old section and the tonic of the new section. In this instance, the common note is C, the third of an A-minor triad (here a dyad) as well as the fifth of an F-major triad. The oboe Cs in measures 96–97 begin the theme of the trio, which follows in F major at measure 98 in a slower tempo and with reduced orchestration. The collapse in measures 87–91, then, not only allowed Mahler to conclude the opening scherzo but also to make a simple transition to a sharply contrasting section.[30]

FRAGMENTATION

Fragmentation is a type of dissolution in which a particular musical texture, melody, or harmony appears to disintegrate and disappear. The music seems to be dispersed or scattered—an effect that differentiates fragmentation from subsidence.

The final pages of Symphony No. 9 exemplify the process of fragmentation, both in measures 144–58,[31] which follow the final primary thematic section, and in measures 159–85, an *adagissimo* coda (Example 4.12), which includes abrupt changes in the texture and pregnant pauses. An authentic cadence in measures 163–64 and a plagal cadence in measures 172–73 prepare the listener for an extended tonic. But Mahler adds a final passage of fragmentation: the long durations, isolated pitches, and thematic fragments of measures 176–85 create the sense of a lingering, fading farewell. The prolonged tonic in measures 183–85, together with the durational augmentation of the turn figure, with reordered pitches, in the viola at measures 184–85 suggests final closure, which comes with durational and dynamic closure in measure 185. As Leonard Bernstein aptly describes it:

> And so we come to the final incredible page. And this page, I think, is the closest we have ever come, in any work of art, to experiencing the very act of dying, of giving it all up. The slowness of this page is terrifying: *Adagissimo,* he writes, the slowest possible musical direction, and then *langsam* (slow), *ersterbend* (dying away), *zögend* (hestitating); and as if all those were not enough to indicate the near stoppage of time, he adds *äußerst langsam* (extremely slow) in the very last bars. It is terrifying, and paralyzing, as the strands of sound disintegrate. We hold on to them, hovering between hope and submission. And one by one, these spidery strands connecting us to life melt away, vanish from our fingers even as we hold them. We cling to them as they dematerialize; we are holding two—

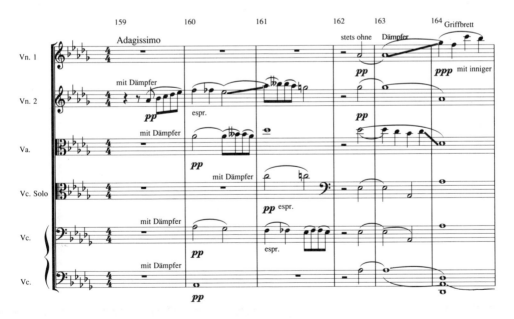

EXAMPLE 4.12. Mahler, Symphony No. 9, IV, mm. 159–85.   *(continued)*

EXAMPLE 4.12 (*cont.*)

then one. One, and suddenly none. For a petrifying moment there is only silence. Then again, a strand, a broken strand, two strands, one . . . none.[32]

Mahler does not use fragmentation very often to create closure, but another example is found in the third movement of Symphony No. 7 (Example 4.13),[33] and the effect is playful rather than profoundly peaceful. Throughout measures 474–504 we hear motives and fragments of themes from the trio section of the movement. In particular, in the upper woodwinds in measures 493–94 we hear all but the last note— the tonic D—of the well-established closing phrase of the trio section.[34] There is a sense of delayed resolution because the timpani begins its motive (measure 495) with a D, but this "resolution" comes after a slight pause and is not in the expected register, thereby contributing to the gesture of fragmentation. In addition to the closing phrase at measure 493, generally abating processes in registral pitch and dynamics at measures 488–92 and 493–500 prepare the listener for final closure, which seems to occur with durational closure in measure 500, except that the suggestion of D minor (the key of the scherzo) in measures 495–501 may lead the listener to think that Mahler will return to the scherzo, or at least extend the closing passage to confirm D minor. Instead in measure 502 Mahler teases us with the prospect of additional closing gestures before a forte D3 in the timpani and a fortissimo tonic major triad in the viola end the movement.

SUBSIDENCE

In order to have a strong closural effect, secondary parameters usually act correspond-ingly. Indeed many of Mahler's closing gestures, especially those involving subsi-dence, are shaped by abatements in at least three of the following parameters: registral pitch, concordance, components, dynamics, and durations. To subside is either (1) "to sink or fall to the bottom; to settle" or (2) "to become quiet; to cease to rage; to be calmed; to become tranquil."[35] Thus, descending pitch patterns and diminishing dynamics are crucial to defining various types of musical subsidence, which in Mahler's works is almost always characterized by decreasing components (usually contributing to a reduction in compound dynamics and an increase in concordance) and often by longer durations. By implication, subsidence refers to a more or less gradual process of dissolution, as opposed to collapse, which is rapid. Accordingly, concordance is the least important parameter for creating subsidence because abating processes in concordance are generally quite short. Gradual abatements in registral pitch, dynamics, components, and durations (usually owing to a slowing tempo) are common, however, and their combined effect can be very striking.

Subsidence is created in many different ways in Mahler's music, and much of the remainder of this chapter is devoted to an examination of the inventive ways in which Mahler produced closure by subsidence. Our focus will be on instances of subsidence that illustrate each of the two definitions quoted above, beginning with an examination of subsidence in which abatements in registral pitch produce the effect of sinking to the bottom or settling, and continuing with discussions of subsidence in which fading dynamics cause the music to become quiet, calm, or tranquil. Of course

EXAMPLE 4.13. Mahler, Symphony No. 7, III, mm. 487–504. Used by permission of G. Schirmer, Inc. on behalf of the copyright owners, Bote & Bock.

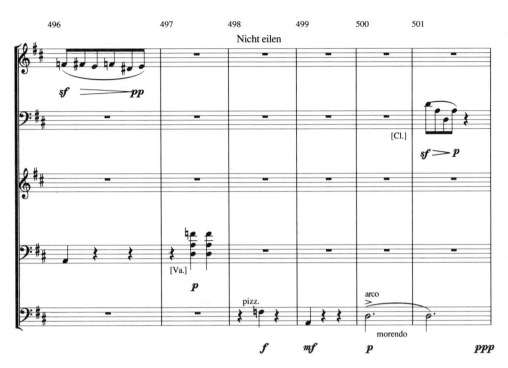

EXAMPLE 4.13 (*cont.*)

EXAMPLE 4.14. Mahler, Symphony No. 1, II, mm. 272–80.

in most instances subsidence is characterized by *both* abating registral pitch and dynamics—sometimes with one process following the other—with the result that the music seems to both fall away and fade away. Moreover, durational closure typically marks the end of a subsiding passage. The division of subsidence into two subcategories is not meant to minimize the importance of the corresponding parameters—most prominently, abating components. It is convenient, however, to distinguish between passages in which decreasing dynamics and components support registral pitch closure, on the one hand, and those in which dynamics and durations are principally responsible for creating closure, on the other hand. That these are not always clearly differentiated strategies of closure only speaks to Mahler's remarkably varied approach to the use of secondary parameters for articulating musical form.

EXAMPLE 4.14 (*cont.*)

Subsidence and Registral Pitch

Mahler's frequent use of extended pedal points is well known, and closure is commonly created in his works when a descending pitch pattern—whether linear, triadic, or sequential—reaches an anticipated conclusion on the pitch of the pedal or some (usually one) octave above it. (See Example 4.7.) The abating process in registral pitch is typically accompanied by decreasing components and dynamics, and such registral pitch closure is often confirmed by durational closure (and often accompanied by tonal pitch closure as well). This kind of subsidence is particularly well suited to closing a tonic prolongation following cadential closure, as is illustrated in Example 4.14 from Symphony No. 1, II. (See also Example 3.12.)

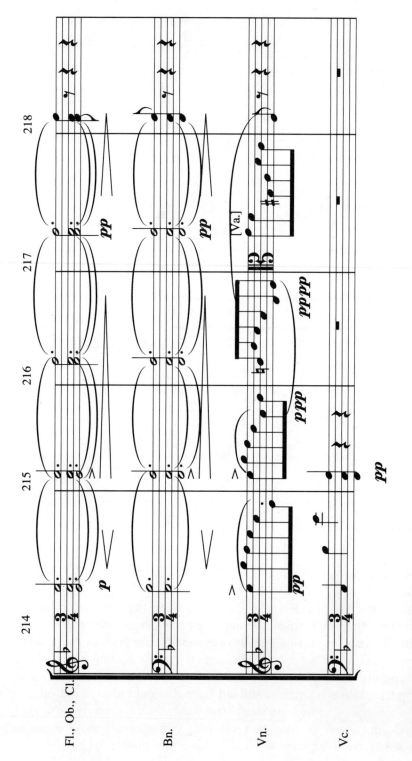

EXAMPLE 4.15. Mahler, Symphony No. 1, II, mm. 214–18.

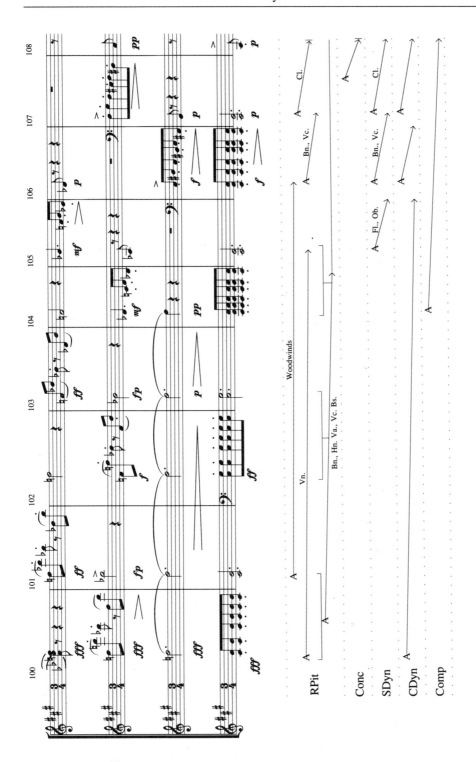

EXAMPLE 4.16. Mahler, Symphony No. 1, II, mm. 100–108.

The perfect authentic cadence in C major at measures 272–74 marks the end of the trio section of the movement, but the extended tonic that follows is closed primarily by abating processes. In particular, a descending pitch pattern beginning in measure 273 "sinks to the bottom," namely the low C pitch of the pedal in measures 273–76. Even though the C-major chord fades to silence in measure 276, the listener remembers the sound and can anticipate that the descending figure in the low strings will come to rest on C2, a point of registral pitch closure that is supported by durational and dynamic closure in the same measure. The rests in measure 280 strengthen the conclusion.

The same basic strategy may give rise to different degrees of closure. For instance, the very parametric processes that create closure in measures 273–80 produced somewhat weaker closure earlier in the trio (Example 4.15). The cadence in F major at measures 214–16 is essentially the same as the one in C major at measures 272–74. Both times the chord resolves before the melody ascends a half step to the tonic. In both instances the tonic harmony is extended, and the extension is closed when a descending registral pitch pattern arrives at the tonic: in measures 215–18 a gradually descending figure in the strings leads from F5 down to F3, and in measures 273–80 a similar pattern in the strings leads from C6 down to C2. As expected, closure is stronger at the end of the entire trio, at least in part because the first prolongation lasts only slightly over three measures whereas the second extends slightly over seven measures, and the descending pitch pattern in measures 215–18 descends two octaves to a pitch an octave above the lowest pedal tone whereas the later one descends four octaves to the lowest pedal tone. Furthermore, the reduction to a single component in measures 277–80 enhances closure. Thus Mahler uses a longer tonic prolongation in measures 273–80 to strengthen closure for the entire trio.

Example 4.14 illustrates a gesture of subsidence following a strong cadence, but Mahler also frequently uses subsidence to conclude sections without a traditional cadence. Moreover, dynamics typically contribute more to creating subsidence than they do in Example 4.14, in which the dynamic abatement in measures 273–80 is rather limited in scope. Consider the end of the B section of the Ländler's rounded binary form in the same movement: five terminally synchronized processes in secondary parameters help create closure. (See the graphs in Example 4.16.) Most of the B section is anchored to a C#2–G#2 double pedal so that tonal harmony is not an important factor in articulating the form. Intensifying processes in dynamics, registral pitch, and components build to a triple fortissimo climax in measure 100, after which abatements in registral pitch and compound dynamics are most effective in creating the climate of prospective closure. Unlike the single descending figure in Example 4.14, though, the abating pitch pattern in this example involves the reiterated C#–G# pedal tones as well as the repeated motives in the violins and high woodwinds. Measures 100–101 are essentially repeated down an octave in the next two measures, and the C#–G# pedal tones are repeated yet an octave lower in measures 104–5, thereby creating the sense of sinking or settling down. A different motive is introduced in the violins at measure 104, and that motive becomes the basis for a continuing abating pitch process in measures 106–8 that leads to registral pitch closure on C♯3 in measure 108. That closure is supported by tonal pitch and concordant closure, and the overall closure is strengthened by terminally synchronized abatements in components and simple and compound dynamics. Moreover, the beginning of measure 108 is stressed as a point of arrival because it initiates another four-measure phrase in the large-scale rhythmic structure of the movement. Nevertheless, the elision with a bridge passage starting in the lower strings prevents a strong overall conclusion, and measures 108–17 lead back to the A part of the Ländler.

Another example of subsidence in which a pattern is repeated in successively lower registers over a sustained pedal is found in Symphony No. 6, III, whose conclusion is given in Example 4.17. The melody in the flute at measures 435–37 is repeated at increasingly lower pitch levels in measures 438–43 (first in the E♭ clarinet, then in the bass clarinet—both shown on the third staff down) while generally descending pitch patterns in other parts, including a shift of the sustained A-minor triad down an octave, contribute to a sense of subsidence and the suggestion

EXAMPLE 4.17. Mahler, Symphony No. 6, III, mm. 435–46.   (continued)

of imminent closure. Increasing durations, decreasing components, and fading dynamics in measures 443–45 reinforce the expectation of closure. The three-measure melody from measures 435–37 is varied and abbreviated in the contrabassoon at measure 443, and finally only the last three notes are repeated to conclude the movement. Tonal pitch, registral pitch, and durational closure in measure 446 is enhanced by the symmetrical relationship between the closing three-note motive in the basses and timpani, on the one hand, and the A2 pitches played in eighth notes at the opening of the movement by the basses, cellos, and timpani, on the other hand.

Just as composers often use deceptive cadences to articulate musical form but deny closure on the tonic, occasionally Mahler will establish a pattern of descending registral pitch in a subsiding passage, but not allow the pitch pattern to reach closure on the anticipated pitch. In Mahler's song *In diesem Wetter* (Example 4.18) the singer concludes the third strophe in measure 91, but the poetic closure is undermined by the clash between the B♭ in the melody and the pedal A, which is sustained throughout

EXAMPLE 4.17 (*cont.*)

measures 86–97. Nevertheless, abatements in registral pitch contribute toward a sense of subsidence in measures 89–92: the A3 pedal, which had been sustained throughout measures 86–89, shifts down an octave in measure 90 and again in measure 92 (where the A2 pitch is still sustained); a generally descending pitch pattern beginning in the right-hand part at measure 89 is repeated at lower pitch levels in succeeding measures; and a chromatically descending pitch pattern in the left hand leads from C♯4 down to B♭2 toward an anticipated A2 on the downbeat of measure 93. The resolution of the B♭2 to A2 would, by octave transfer, resolve the singer's concluding B♭, but B♭2 is not resolved to A2 in measure 93.[36] The implication of concordant closure on an octave A is realized in measure 93, but the resolution is deceptive because the unexpected register weakens the sense of a conclusion. On the other hand, the A4 pitch resolves the singer's B♭4 in its proper register, and that resolution is confirmed by the descending chromatic line from C to A in the right-hand part in measures 96–97.

EXAMPLE 4.17 (*cont.*)

EXAMPLE 4.18. Mahler, *Kindertotenlieder: In diesem Wetter,* mm. 89–97.

There are other instances in Mahler's works in which a tonic or a dominant pedal underlies a passage and a descending scalar pattern reaches conclusion on the pedal tone or an octave thereof, often moving through the flatted second scale degree to the tonic or from the flatted sixth degree to the dominant. Near the end of the second movement of *Das klagende Lied,* there are subsiding passages in measures 404–23 (beginning at rehearsal number 77) and again in 451–80 (beginning at rehearsal number 81; measures 461–80 are given in Example 4.19). Three dominant pedals (E1, E2, E3) undergird both passages, which begin with a fortissimo climax on a ninth chord (an E major ninth at measure 404, an E minor ninth with raised seventh at measure 451). In both cases the music slowly sinks to the pedal tones sustained in the

EXAMPLE 4.19. Mahler, *Das klagende Lied,* II, mm. 461–80.   (*continued*)

EXAMPLE 4.19 (*cont.*)

timpani, cellos, and basses. Both times the subsidence is particularly supportive of the text: "O Leide, weh'!" in measures 404–11 and "Weh'! Die alten Mauern sinken!" in measures 451–68. Concordant, registral pitch, and tonal pitch closure are supported by diminishing dynamics (*ff* down to *pp* or *ppp*) and decreasing components.[37]

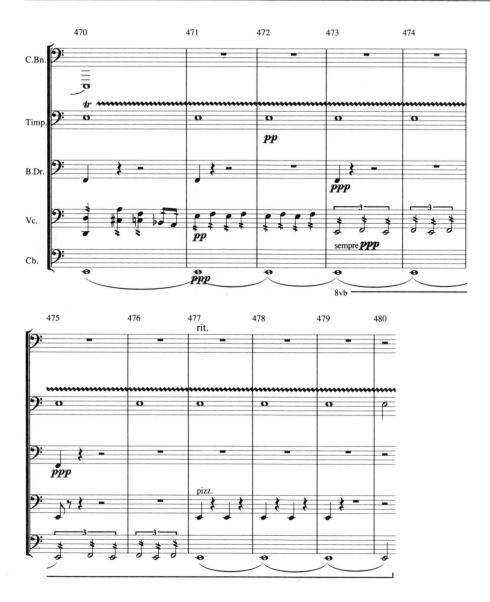

EXAMPLE 4.19 (*cont.*)

Mahler often uses gestures of subsidence following a fortissimo climax near the end of a movement.[38] In the second movement of *Das klagende Lied* he uses two such passages at measures 404 and 451; the second of these climaxes is stronger not only because it is longer, but also because it begins more forcefully with the whole orchestra (in measure 451) and with a more discordant harmony. This type of compositional planning, namely the use of a series of intensification-abatement structures with each intensification greater than the last, is familiar to listeners of late nineteenth-century music. Leonard Ratner has described the procedure as a "dynamic curve" that was "an important resource for building structure in nineteenth-century and early twentieth-century music."[39]

The climax of the third movement in the Second Symphony is followed by a gesture of subsidence much like the ones we have been considering, but with an important difference. As in other movements, intensifying processes in several parameters lead to a tremendous climax (measure 465), the so-called "cry of despair," after which the music subsides. In this case, however, the harmony, which consists of a B♭-minor triad over a C pedal, is prolonged until measure 473 (Example 3.12), whereupon a descending scalar pattern leads from B♭ down to C while the low winds and timpani sustain the pedal C in three registers. As in both gestures of subsidence in *Das klagende Lied*, in which the music descends to the pedal note from the half step above, here the scale pattern descends through D♭ to C, though the melody in the first violins and flutes descends less than an octave to C6, which is four octaves above the lowest pedal tone. Closure is still strong in large part because of the use of ♭II$^{6\sharp}$ as a substitute dominant in measure 480, which clearly differentiates Example 3.12 from the others we have considered above.

When a half step is the final descending interval in a subsiding pitch pattern, the penultimate harmony can be rather tensive if it is sustained for any significant duration, as it is in measure 480 where the ♭II$^{6\sharp}$ chord is discordant with the tonic pedal. In a significant sense, then, the ♭II$^{6\sharp}$ chord has the same role as a dominant in a traditional cadence: it is a local point of *climax* that resolves directly to the tonic.[40] Therefore, the particular compositional strategy illustrated in Example 3.12 enables Mahler to combine abating closure, which is created by the parameters of registral pitch and concordance in measure 481, with his own version of cadential closure based on the principle of tension and release characteristic of the traditional tonal cadence. This may account for the fact that the descending pitch pattern does not sink down to the pedal tone or an octave above the pedal. That kind of abating conclusion may not be necessary when a ♭II$^{6\sharp}$–I cadence is employed. The effect of the closure in Example 3.12 is quite different, then, from that in Example 4.16, for instance. The closure in measure 481 is more active and more emphatic, characteristics that may explain why the resolution in measure 481 is followed by a long prolongation of the tonic to measure 517, a prolongation that slowly fades away, thus allowing more of the tension to be released. The extension begins with the fortissimo entrance of the cellos and basses at the end of measure 480, an entrance that promotes mobility despite the simple durational closure in the violins and winds at measure 482.

It is not uncommon for Mahler to elide the end of a subsidence, or any dissolution, with the beginning of another passage. Often the timpani or bass drum provides ongoing motion at the point of elision. Consider the conclusion of the third scherzo section in the second movement of Symphony No. 4 (Example 4.20). This

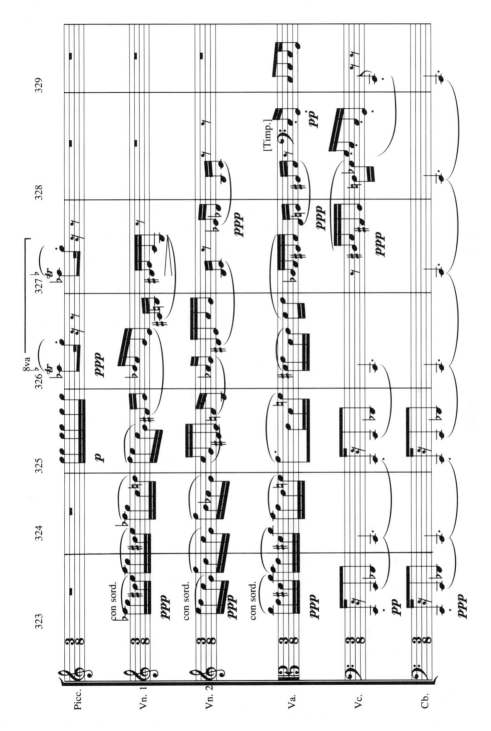

EXAMPLE 4.20. Mahler, Symphony No. 4, II, mm. 323–29.

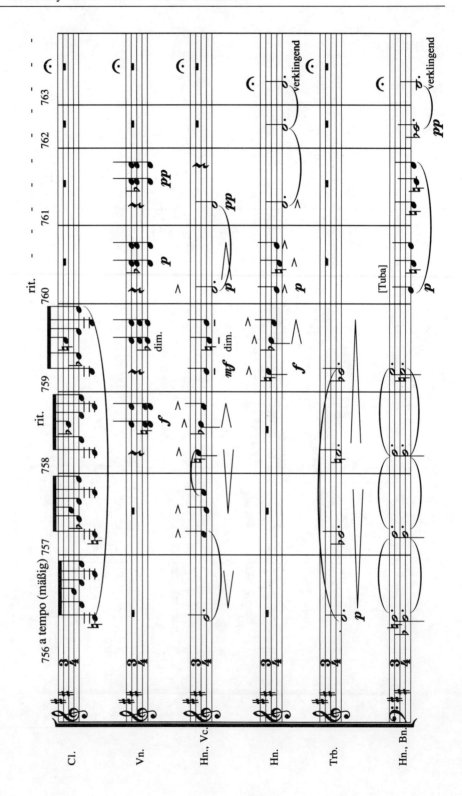

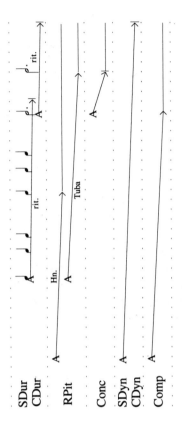

EXAMPLE 4.21. Mahler, Symphony No. 5, III, mm. 756–63.

abatement ends a tonic prolongation following a perfect authentic cadence in measures 313–14. Unlike the examples just considered, this passage does not follow any climax, and in fact dynamics do not vary much throughout the passage except to the extent that decreasing components result in decreasing compound dynamics. On the other hand, an abating process in registral pitch (the generally descending pitch patterns in the first violins at measures 324–27 and the cellos in measures 327–29) is terminally synchronized with durational and concordant closure, as well as tonal pitch closure, at the beginning of measure 329. The sinking pitch pattern in the first violins and cellos descends through the tonic triad from G5 in measure 324 to C2, the pitch of the pedal, in measure 329. The use of triadic motion is of course a traditional prolonging strategy, one that reflects the importance of the primary parameters in this movement.[41] The ongoing timpani part prevents component closure at measure 329, and leads into the coda.

The passage that closes the final trio section of the scherzo from the Fifth Symphony (Example 4.21) also comes just before the coda. The example illustrates that dynamics may be as important as registral pitch in subsidence. Accordingly, the calming effect of dynamics is probably as significant as the effect of falling to the bottom. Indeed, unlike previous examples of subsidence, the pedal tone is in a middle register (D4) and is only extended for four measures; the tuba figure sinks to an octave *below* the pedal. The tuba melody is of course a varied repetition of the horn melody in measures 759–61 (staff 4), and in measures 758–60 (staff 3). The tuba figure fills the gap between G and D in the melody, and approaches the final D through E♭, thereby creating a discordant major seventh with the pedal.[42] Again the process in concordance, that of building to a local climax that is resolved immediately, seems modeled after the tonal cadence, but the entire process is part of an overall dissolution in measures 756–63. Abatements in registral pitch, concordance, and components are terminally synchronized at measure 763, and dynamic and durational closure at the end of the measure considerably strengthen the repose produced by concordant and registral pitch closure on the first beat of the measure. This striking gesture of subsidence is truly the "calm before the storm"; the coda builds quickly from a pianissimo to a triple fortissimo, and the movement ends *fff* with an implied authentic cadence.

Our final example of subsidence and registral pitch comes from the end of the opening movement of Symphony No. 5 (Example 4.22). As in Example 4.21, decreasing dynamics and descending registral pitch in Example 4.22 play equally

EXAMPLE 4.22. Mahler, Symphony No. 5, I, mm. 369–401.   (*continued*)

EXAMPLE 4.22 (*cont.*)

EXAMPLE 4.22 (*cont.*)

important roles in a gesture of subsidence, which in this case follows a triple fortissimo climax—*the* climax of the movement—in measures 369–70. The movement has a composed-out rounded binary form in which a coda based on A material takes the place of a final A section, thus: A A′ B A″ B′ Coda. The movement opens with a trumpet fanfare, and the return of that fanfare at the end of measure 232 articulates the beginning of the A″ section. In a similar fashion, the forte entrance of the trumpet fanfare at the end of measure 376 in Example 4.22 (staff 3) articulates the beginning of the coda, but the articulation is weakened by continuing abatements in registral pitch and dynamics. Diminishing dynamics in measures 370–92 are especially effective in creating a sense of growing calm as the music fades from *fff* to *pp*. Even the trumpet fanfare becomes more and more subdued in measure 383–92, after which the music remains pianissimo.

From measure 392 to 401, however, descending pitch patterns are most influential in lessening tension. Of course abatements in both registral pitch and components contribute to the gesture of subsidence, though the parameters are not synchronized

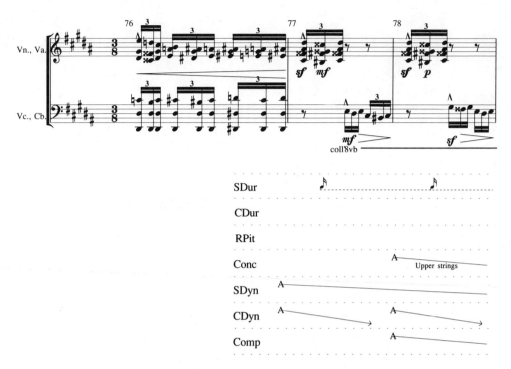

EXAMPLE 4.23. Mahler, Symphony No. 2, II, mm. 76–85.

throughout. Components are gradually reduced from the eleven at measure 369 to one, the solo trumpet, in measures 391–92. With regard to registral pitch, descending conjunct lines are found in measures 370–90 (A5 to A3 in the violins), 380–90 (E3 to A1 in the low strings and bassoons), and 390–401 (F♯5 to C♯3 in the trumpet and low strings). The sense of sinking to the bottom is accentuated by the chromatic descent in the lowest instruments beginning in measure 377. Like Example 4.21, this passage does not have one prolonged pedal anchoring the subsiding gesture. Instead, Mahler abandons the E pedal at measure 377, and at the same time that the falling bass line contributes to a sense of subsidence, the music effects a transition to the tonic chord in measure 401. Example 4.22, then, is a remarkable instance of a passage that combines both transition and closing functions.

The solo trumpet fanfare that began the movement returns at the end of measure 396, and its return creates a symmetry that suggests final closure is imminent. The trumpet's reiterated C♯ implies C♯ is a goal for the descending figure in the bass, which descends a half step to resolve a major seventh to an octave. Thus, tonal pitch and concordant closure mark the end of the subsidence following the climax in measure 369.[43]

So far the examples of subsidence that we have discussed—subsidence that creates the sense of sinking to the bottom, or settling—have illustrated Mahler's inventive methods of adapting a basic compositional strategy to particular situa-

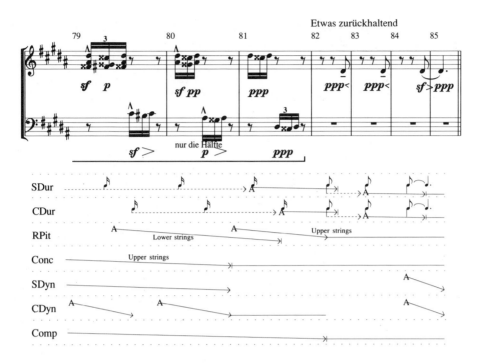

EXAMPLE 4.23 (*cont.*)

tions.[44] The same creative variety of closing passages is found in examples of subsidence that are defined more by dynamics and duration than by registral pitch and duration.

Subsidence and Dynamics

We have already seen instances in which the music becomes quiet and calm, including instances in which the music ceases to rage—when it subsides after a climax. In this section we will focus attention on gestures of subsidence in which dynamics and duration play a crucial role, and though registral pitch is often abating there is generally no registral pitch closure. Most of the time a musical passage becomes quiet and tranquil because of a prominent diminuendo, typically supported by abatements in components, durations, and registral pitch. In Mahler's music this kind of subsidence typically occurs in a passage characterized by static harmony or grounded in an extended pedal.

There are a few circumstances, however, in which an abating passage seems to become calm in large part because it is reduced, or contracted, to a fragment of what it was—what might be called a *reduction*. Consider, for instance, closing passages from the ends of the two trio sections in the second movement of Symphony No. 2.

The movement is a five-part Ländler and trio in which the two sections alternate, the Ländler in A♭ major and the trio in G♯ minor. The conclusions of the trio sections, which are quite similar, are given in Examples 4.23 and 4.24; in both, a one-measure unit is reduced to a single D♯, a pitch then reinterpreted as E♭, the fifth of A♭ major and the initial pitch of the Ländler theme. In measures 86–92 and 210–16 (not shown in the examples) Mahler reverses the process of dissolution by repeating the E♭ while gradually adding successive pitches in the A♭-major chord below it, to build toward a restatement of the Ländler theme. Thus, as in many of the examples of dissolution, Mahler uses reduction as a means of concluding one section as well as providing a way of leading directly into the next section.

In Examples 4.23 and 4.24 descending pitch patterns, increasing concordance, diminishing dynamics, decreasing components, and increasing durations all point toward closure following passages characterized by sixteenth-note triplets and a crescendo toward a local climax (measures 74–77 and 193–96, respectively; not shown in the examples). There are significant, and interesting, differences between the two passages, however. Only strings play in measures 76–85, whereas measures 196–201 include wind instruments (flute, oboe, clarinet, bassoon, and horn). The abatements are generally more pronounced in Example 4.24, where the dynamic level in the upper strings, for instance, begins at fortissimo in measure 196 and decreases to pianissimo in measure 209. In Example 4.23, on the other hand, the dynamic range is only *mf* to *ppp*. The abating processes in both examples are supported by a process of reduction, though it is less explicit in Example 4.23 than it is in Example 4.24. In the latter example, after the opening pattern has been reduced to a pair of triplets in measure 205, both the pitch and durational structures of the sixteenth-note triplets are clearly broken down in measures 206–9. The pitch structure is reduced to a single pitch by eliminating the first and subsequently the second pitch of the pattern. The sixteenth-note triplet pattern is destroyed in measures 206–9 as well. The reduction to a single staccato eighth note D in measure 209 is dramatic, both in view of the resources available to Mahler and the resources he actually began the passage with in measure 196. The dissolution in Example 4.24, then, is particularly effective in supporting durational closure in measure 209.

A somewhat different example of reduction is found in the third movement of Symphony No. 6 (Example 4.25). The general abatement in registral pitch in measures 168–72 is strengthened by basically diminishing compound dynamics and the reduction to a single component at measure 172. (The forte entrance of the timpani at the end of measure 172 begins a transition to the second part of the trio.) The overlapping repetitions of the motive at lower and lower pitch levels in measures

EXAMPLE 4.24. Mahler, Symphony No. 2, II, mm. 196–209.

EXAMPLE 4.25. Mahler, Symphony No. 6, III, mm. 162–72.

167–72 makes it seem as though the passage were falling apart, especially since the motive is all that is left from the first violin theme in measures 162–65:

It is noteworthy that the first part of the trio does not end with strong traditional harmonic closure in F major at measures 165, 167, or 168, but rather with an abating closing gesture in measures 167–72 that simultaneously makes a transition to A

EXAMPLE 4.25 (*cont.*)

minor. The lack of durational closure in measure 165 and the ongoing durational processes in measures 167–68 undermine strong cadential closure.[45]

Strict processes of reduction are relatively rare in Mahler's works.[46] They constitute only a small segment of a broad category of subsiding passages that grow quiet and calm because of fading dynamics, decreasing components, and longer durations. Falling pitch patterns may also contribute to the sense of dying away. Often such a subsiding passage closes a passage that prolongs a particular harmony— notably a tonic prolongation following cadential closure—and consequently they are most common in the early songs and Symphonies 1 through 4, in which pedal points and cadential closure are common. Example 4.6, from the end of the introduction to the first movement of the First Symphony, is a case in point. Frequently these subsiding passages do not follow a dynamic climax, but rather fade from piano or pianissimo either to the softest possible dynamic level or to silence.[47]

Thus, in a given context even a modest dynamic abatement can help generate a sense that a passage is on the wane. Consider Example 4.26, from the end of the Fourth Symphony. Here durational and dynamic closure in measure 184 conclude the tonic prolongation that follows a perfect full cadence in measures 161–63. Cadential closure is confirmed by repeated $V_{(7)}$–I progressions in measures 173–76 and the arrival of tonal pitch closure on E4 in the vocal part at measure 174 (not shown in the example). The tempo slows somewhat in the final seven measures ("sich Zeit lassen!" Mahler instructs the harpist), and gradually parts drop out until component closure is achieved when the music falls to a lone E1 in measure 182. Thus, this example of subsidence combines the effect of sinking to the bottom with the calming and quieting effect of longer durations and fading dynamics. Durational closure at measure 184 is followed by dynamic closure: the arrival at silence. It is significant, too, that the concluding E-major section of the movement both begins and ends with the sounding of E1 in the harp and basses. In fact, measures 178–83 are a kind of retrograde variation of measures 122–25, which introduced the E-major section. That symmetry further strengthens final closure, and helps make the conclusion persuasive even though G major, rather than E major, has been treated as the tonal center for much of the movement, and indeed the symphony. The powerful combination of repeated cadential closure and effective abating closure is entirely convincing.

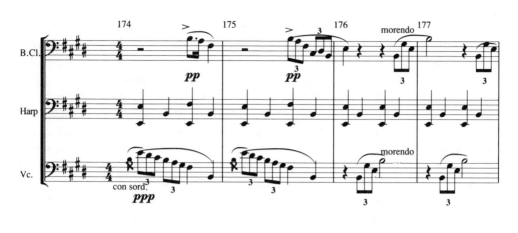

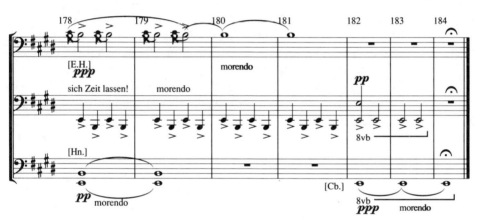

EXAMPLE 4.26. Mahler, Symphony No. 4, IV, mm. 174–84.

Another subsidence that fades to silence comes from the very end of the recapitulation in the opening movement of Symphony No. 2 (Example 4.27). The secondary theme is recapitulated in E major at measure 362, and it reaches closure with a quiet plagal cadence in measures 369–70, after which there is an extended prolongation of E major over an E2 pedal. At first a sense of subsidence is most clearly felt as a result of a gradually falling pitch pattern in the violins in measures 372–82. After the discordant harmony of measure 383 resolves to the E-major triad in measure 384, however, a potent combination of factors contribute to creating a sense of tranquility and an expectation of imminent closure: the reiteration of the E-major chord, the slowing tempo (note the "Immer langsamer" indication in measure 384), the repetition of the viola melody from measures 384–85 an octave lower in the cellos at measures 386–87, and especially the fading dynamics. Mahler writes "bis zum gänzlichen Aufhören" ("to the point of completely subsiding") in the score. The lower parts drop out in measure 388 and reduce the compound dynamic level to a mere whisper. The long abatement in compound durations is terminally synchronized with the anticipated dynamic closure at the end of measure 391, which is the strongest point of abating closure in the passage and concludes the gesture of subsidence.[48]

Nevertheless, abating closure at measure 391 is weakened by the unstable tonal harmony. With regard to tonal harmony, measures 388–91 amount to a transition from the E major of measures 362–88 to the C minor of the coda. As in Example 4.22, then, this passage combines the functions of closing and transition. The music continues to wane even as the shifting harmonies suggest E major, then E minor, then E♭ major—or, considering the context of the work, C minor. Note the reversal of roles: whereas secondary parameters had been used throughout the nineteenth century to promote mobility at points of strong cadential closure, here unstable tonal harmony—a syntactic, primary parameter—promotes mobility at a point of strong abating closure created by the secondary parameters of dynamics, compound duration, concordance, registral pitch, and components. The combined effect of the many corresponding parameters in this passage is probably sufficient to create persuasive closure despite the changing harmony.

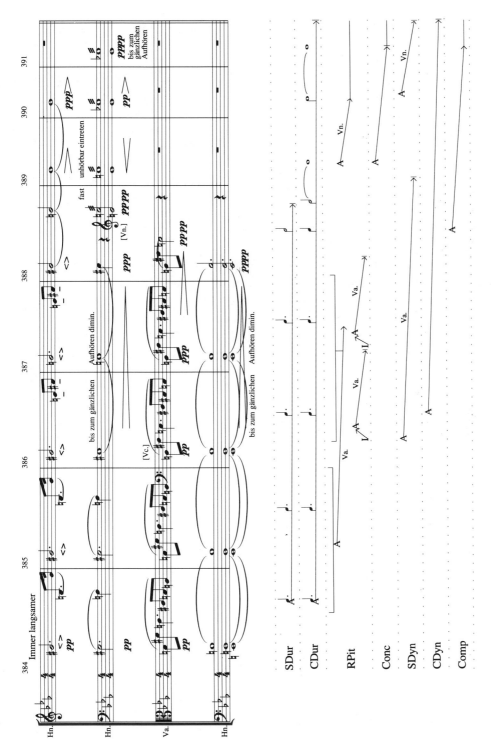

EXAMPLE 4.27. Mahler, Symphony No. 2, I, mm. 384–91.

Example 4.28 presents a rather different passage that also functions as both a conclusion and a transition. The third movement of Symphony No. 4 has an overall A B A′ B′ A″ form, and in this passage Mahler brings the B′ section to a close on an F♯ sonority while providing a transition to the A″ section in the tonic key of G major (measure 222). An intensification in measures 202–9 leads to a fortissimo climax in measure 210.[49] Mahler asserts and prolongs F♯ minor (and then F♯ major) in measures 210–20, where abatements in registral pitch, dynamics, and components imply prospective closure. As in Example 4.27, this gesture of subsidence is initially defined primarily by descending pitch patterns, and then chiefly by fading dynamics and augmenting durations. Durational closure occurs in measure 218, but the abatement in dynamics continues to measure 221, at which point there is dynamic, component, and concordant closure on the unison D3.[50] The lack of durational closure and harmonic stability, however, undermines any sense of strong abating closure.

Retrospectively the listener realizes that the D3 pitch, originally understood as a neighbor note to C♯, is reinterpreted as the root of an implied dominant chord (with augmented fifth) that resolves to the tonic G-major chord in measure 222, and further that the alternating A3 and A♯3 pitches in the violas and second violins become part of a chromatic line ascending to B3 in measure 222. The listener also understands in retrospect that the durational closure on the F♯-major chord of measure 218 was the strongest point of abating closure in a passage that continued to fade through measure 221. Thus, in this passage Mahler dovetails a closing section with a transition. His procedure is not much different from that in the last few measures of Example 4.11 where he dissolves a chord to a single note that leads into the next section. Here Mahler dissolves the musical fabric to a single note, not a part of the extended F♯ triad, in order to effect a transition to the next section.

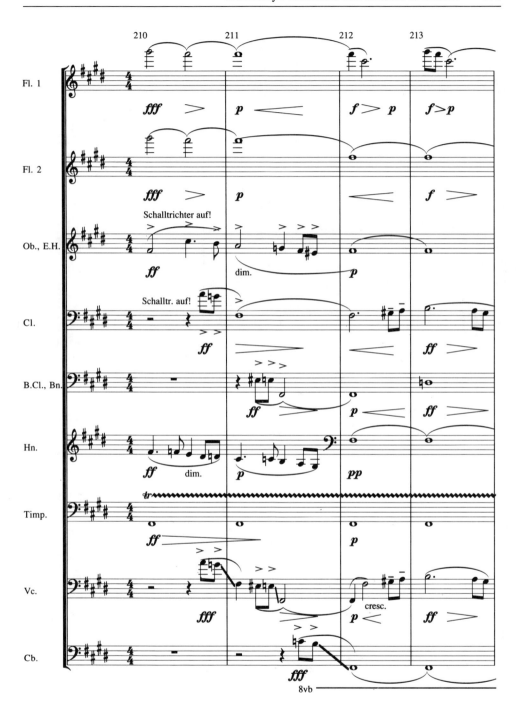

EXAMPLE 4.28. Mahler, Symphony No. 4, III, mm. 210–22.   (*continued*)

EXAMPLE 4.28 (*cont.*)

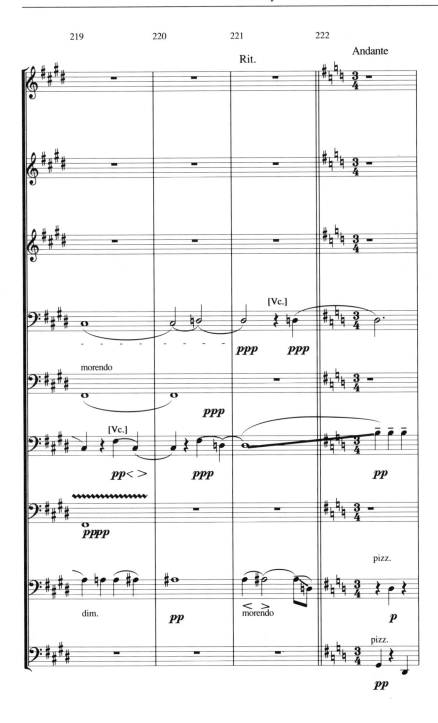

EXAMPLE 4.28 (*cont.*)

Sometimes a musical passage is reduced to a single note by a more or less steady decrease in the number of components, and when such a process is combined with diminishing dynamics and durational closure, as in Example 4.29, the resulting closure can be particularly effective. In this instance a sense of growing calm is created primarily by decreasing components and dynamics, though it is an abating process in durations that secures closure on F in measure 389. Again the conclusion of the passage leads directly into the following section. The singer articulates the beginning of the next passage with her entrance "Er sprach," ending on the very same F just released by the oboe. The overall effect is that of a single prolonged F in measures 389–90. Interestingly enough, the compound duration in measure 390 is longer than that in measure 389, so the singer both begins a new passage and provides compound durational closure for the previous one.

Durational closure often concludes the types of subsidence we have been considering in this section and durational augmentation can be an important part of

EXAMPLE 4.29. Mahler, *Das Lied von der Erde*, VI, mm. 386–90.

EXAMPLE 4.30. Mahler, Symphony No. 3, VI, mm. 182–97.

the subsiding gesture, as illustrated in Example 4.30 from the finale to the Third Symphony. The passage is one of three in the movement (measures 79–91, 182–97, and 238–44) in which gestures of subsidence follow a climax and precede a return of the primary theme. In each case a prolonged harmony is gradually reduced to a single component, and decrescendos from *ff* down to *pp* or *ppp* help create subsidence. The passage in Example 4.30 releases tension after climactic, increasingly discordant *ff* chords in measures 178–81; in effect, the music ceases to rage.

The B♭–G–A–B♭ motive in the horns at measures 180–82 is repeated several times in measures 182–92, notably with augmented durations first in the horns in measures 182–85 and then in the bassoons and brass in measures 186–92 (shown in the bottom staff of Example 4.30). Overlapping statements of the motive are played at increasingly lower octaves in the same measures (see the bottom staff in measures 182–85, second staff up in 184–87, bottom staff in 186–92). All of this contributes to the implication of imminent closure, as does the diminuendo from *ff* to *ppp*. Component closure on the unison C♯ on the second beat of measure 194 and durational closure (see the top staff) in measure 196 realize that implication. Note that abating closure in this example (as well as in measures 90–91 and 242–44) is produced in a context of static tonal harmony and is not supported by tonal pitch closure.

In measures 182–92 of Example 4.30 the most prominent abating process is the augmenting durations, which give the listener a sense that the music is slowing to a halt. In the last part of Example 4.30, on the other hand, a reduction in components plays a crucial role, as it has in the other examples of dissolution we have considered thus far.[51] As we have pointed out, however, abating durations create closure in Mahler's works far more often than components or any other secondary parameter, and in fact there are many occasions in which a substantial abatement in durations— as in the beginning of Example 4.30—leads to closure *without* a substantial abatement in components. Such conclusions are characterized by a sense of slackening tempo—a sense that the music is becoming more tranquil as it slowly comes to a standstill. Typically such conclusions come at the ends of works, where harmony is static, especially after durational augmentation of some motive leads to closure on a chord marked with a fermata; subsequently the music often fades to silence. Mahler commonly writes "morendo" or "gänzlich ersterbend" in the score.

Consider the close of the third movement in Symphony No. 4 (Example 4.31). Following an authentic cadence in measures 338–41, the *pppp* melody in the second violins falls from F♯6 in measure 338 to G4 in measure 344, thereby suggesting final closure on the tonic G is close at hand. However the movement ends on a dominant harmony, with the leading tone of the scale in the top voice. Thus, secondary parameters are responsible for final closure. The repetition of the ♩ ♩ ♩ | ♩ ♩ motive with gradually longer durations in measures 343–46 (measures 338 and following are marked "Allmählich wieder zurückhaltend") and greatly augmented durations in measures 347–50 create a sense that the passage is slowly coming to a stop. As the basses and then clarinets drop out in measures 351–52, compound timbres become purer, compound dynamics softer, and compound durations longer. Final closure is created by terminally synchronized abatements in dynamics and compound duration, and is enhanced by the abatement in compound timbre. All but one of the string parts in measures 352–53 are harmonics, which together with the flute sounds produce a nearly pure compound timbre. (That timbre contrasts sharply with the rich string timbre of measures 338–43.) The music fades to silence on a dominant chord that is resolved by the tonic chord that opens the next movement.

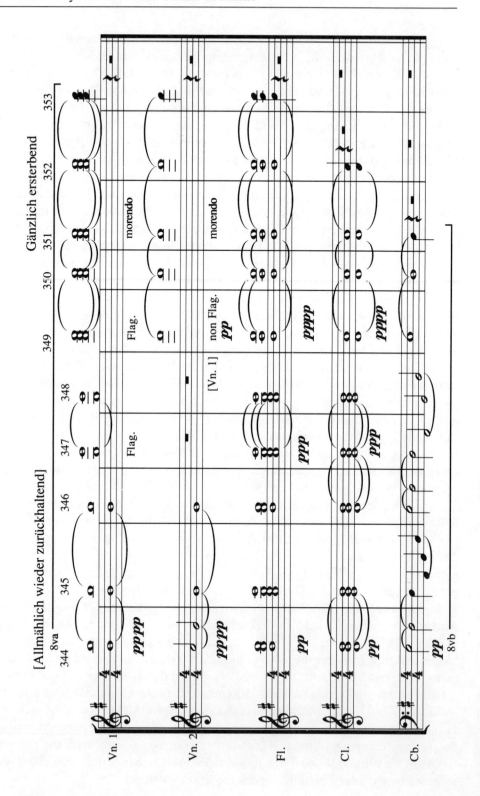

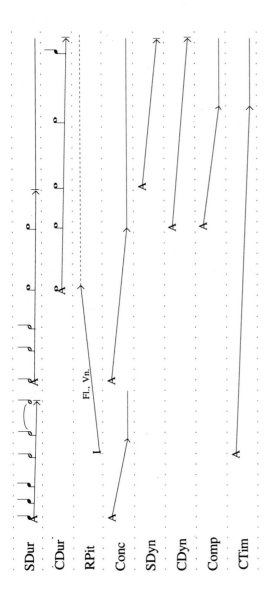

EXAMPLE 4.31. Mahler, Symphony No. 4, III, mm. 344–53.

The kind of subsiding gesture given in Example 4.31 can be found within a movement as well. Example 4.32 gives such an instance. A pianissimo F-major sonority is prolonged in measures 318–29, which are undergirded by a double pedal of F2/C2. A descending pitch pattern in the lower strings at measures 318–21 (not shown in the example) is the first prominent closing gesture, but the augmenting durations and diminishing dynamics in measures 323–29 are most important for closing the passage. Measure 321 is marked "Zurückhalten," and the passage clearly slows to a standstill with the augmenting durations growing from eighth-note triplets in measure 323 to the tied duration of measures 328–29. Durational and dynamic closure in the latter measures are responsible for concluding the passage, which completes an orchestral extension following the alto and tenor soloists' refrain "O Leide, Leide!" at measures 306–7. The refrain itself is a sign of closure, since it comes at the end of each strophe of the poem.

EXAMPLE 4.32. Mahler, *Das klagende Lied,* I, mm. 323–31.

The gesture of subsidence in Example 4.32 seems particularly appropriate after the soloists sing of the minstrel's music in measures 302–7: "Es klingt so traurig und doch so schön! Wer's hört, der möcht' vor Leid vergehn! O Leide, Leide!" ("It sounds so sad and yet so beautiful! Whoever hears it might wish to die of sorrow! Oh sorrow, sorrow!"). The E♭-minor chord in the winds at measure 330 heralds the next section.

There are many other instances of subsiding gestures in Mahler's music, especially in his vocal works, that illustrate the slowing and quieting effect we have been examining.[52] Letting the music slowly draw to a conclusion and then fade away to silence seems to be a favorite strategy for Mahler to use in closing entire vocal works and sections of vocal works in which the text is sad or tragic.

Though this kind of subsidence usually occurs in a concordant and harmonically stable context, there are exceptions. For instance, augmenting durations and fading

EXAMPLE 4.32 (cont.)

dynamics mark the end of the second thematic section in the recapitulation of Symphony No. 1, IV, even though the harmony in measures 496–533 is discordant— and dissonant—throughout (Example 4.33). The passage in Example 4.33 comes at the end of a long dominant prolongation that begins in measure 436, where we first hear the dominant pedal that is sustained until measure 555. The dominant pedal is a high-level dissonance that implies a resolution to the tonic. The music builds to a discordant and dissonant *fff* climax in measure 496, after which falling pitch patterns, diminishing dynamics, and dwindling components lessen the tension. The harmony is prolonged for such a long time and at such soft dynamic levels that much of the tension inherent in the discordant harmony is dissipated. The dissonance remains, however, and the listener expects eventual resolution of the dominant pedal to the tonic. (Extremely long pedal tones are a common device in the symphony, though, so the dominant pedal is not necessarily a sign of imminent closure in measures 502–32 any more than it was in previous measures.)

In the measures following 502 the augmented durational pattern in the flutes and oboes—that is, the ever-slower E–D motion—leads to durational closure at measure 517.[53] A continuing dynamic abatement suggests that the chord may fade to silence, but as it does there is a *ff* entrance of the violas at measure 519 that foreshadows a return of the primary theme. The prominent durational augmentation and the dynamic abatement from *fff* to *pp* in the violas at measures 520–29 shape the end of the section even while the violas are repeating the head motive of the primary theme. Thus the motivic structure is anticipatory at the same time the fading dynamics and augmented durations suggest closure. Here again, Mahler combines the functions of closing and transition. The sustained discord and dissonance of Example 4.33 dissolves to the dominant pedal as the primary theme returns in the violins and cellos at measures 533–34, where strong closure is avoided because the high-level dissonance—the dominant—is not resolved.

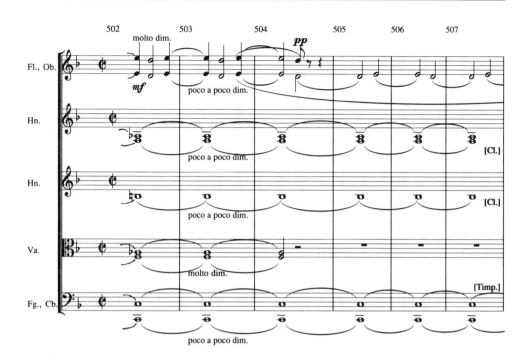

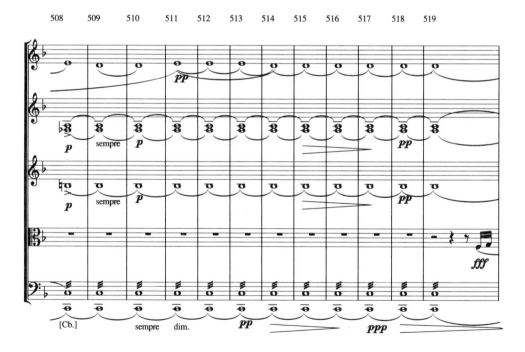

EXAMPLE 4.33. Mahler, Symphony No. 1, IV, mm. 502–34.   (*continued*)

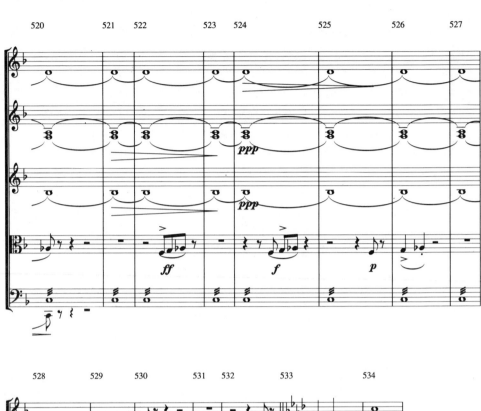

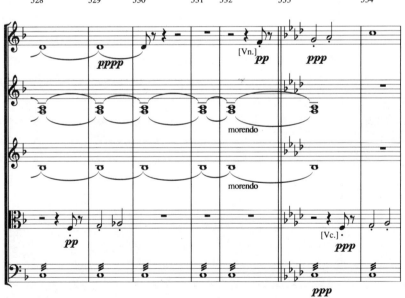

EXAMPLE 4.33 (cont.)

Dynamics, components, and durations feature most prominently in the creation of closure in the gestures of subsidence we have examined in this section, though abating processes in registral pitch also play a significant role in many passages. It should be clear that both abating registral pitch and abating dynamics generally help define a gesture of subsidence even though one or the other may be most prominent in a particular passage. And it is quite evident that the extent to which one or another parameter is prominent in a dissolution has a significant effect on both the character and the potency of the closure that is created.

*   *   *

OTHER STRATEGIES

Most of this chapter has been devoted to a consideration of different types of dissolution, especially the frequent and greatly varied gestures of subsidence. We now turn our attention briefly to some other strategies of closure using secondary parameters.

Since we are primarily interested in studying the ways in which Mahler created closure by using secondary parameters rather than relying on cadential closure, we have concentrated on examples in which processes in secondary parameters are chiefly responsible for creating closure, or instances in which abatements in secondary parameters conclude a tonic prolongation following a traditional cadence. Of course one can find many examples where Mahler combines convincing abating closure with traditional tonal closure, as seen in Example 4.34a, the strong cadential gesture from the opening measures of Symphony No. 7, IV. The F in the solo violin at measure 4 not only creates tonal pitch closure, but also completes a gap-fill structure with the return to the initial pitch of the ascending leap that began the movement. Moreover, a decrescendo is terminally synchronized with the tonal and registral pitch closure in measure 4, where there is also tonal harmonic closure and simple durational closure. The closing phrase of measures 1–4 returns to articulate subdivisions of the A section of the movement at measures 23–26, 35–38, and 51–54. In measures 35–38 closure is strengthened by an abating process in concordance that is highly synchronized with the abatements in dynamics and registral pitch. The cadential phrase also returns to begin the A′ section at measure 260, and is reiterated (in the solo cello) for the last time in measures 292–95 (Example 4.34b). As in measures 35–38, a process of generally increasing concordance in measures 292–95 reinforces closure in measure 295, where there is an elision with the next phrase.

Sometimes cadential closure is terminally synchronized with concordant closure, or even concordant and component closure as in Example 4.35 from Symphony No. 4. Abating dynamics and durational closure fortify the conclusion in measure 22. The same gesture is repeated in varied form to close phrases at measures 34, 63, 133, and 145 of the second movement.[54] In Symphony No. 2, III (e.g., measures 27–31)

EXAMPLE 4.34. Mahler, Symphony No. 7, IV: (*a*) mm. 1–4; (*b*) mm. 292–95. Used by permission of
G. Schirmer, Inc. on behalf of the copyright owners, Bote & Bock.

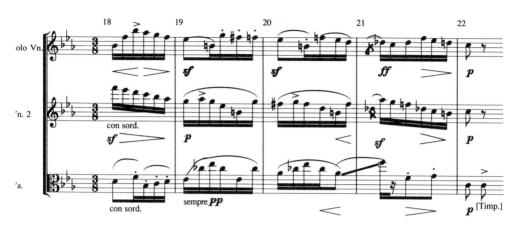

EXAMPLE 4.35. Mahler, Symphony No. 4, II, mm. 18–22.

and *Des Antonius von Padua Fischpredigt* (e.g., measures 23–27), Mahler uses the same strategy to close a phrase where there is no authentic cadence, but rather a descending progression of triads V–IV–III–♭II that lead to an octave on the tonic.

On occasion, as in Example 4.36, cadential closure is strengthened by a terminally synchronized dynamic process that fades away to the tonic. There is an elision in measure 84 with a phrase in the strings, but the phrase ending in the woodwinds is very clear. The woodwinds' phrase fades to an extremely soft dynamic at the beginning of measure 84, where only the piccolo and clarinet remain. The closure in measure 84 is strengthened by the descending pitch patterns in the woodwinds in measures 81–84, especially the descent from D♭6 to D♭5 in the piccolo.

As observed in chapter 3, the use of an extreme dynamic level—either very soft or very loud—can signal to the listener that the end has arrived. In sharp contrast to the fading dynamics in Example 4.36, *fff* dynamics help create emphatic closure at the end of the development section in Symphony No. 2, I. Intensifications in several different parameters begin in measure 320 and build to a *fff* climax on a V_{13} chord in measure 328. The resolution of the dominant chord to the *fff* tonic in measure 329 both closes the development and marks the beginning of the recapitulation.

Secondary parameters also contribute to creating emphatic closure at the ends of the first and third movements of Symphony No. 3. The first movement concludes with a loud, brief coda (measures 867–75) that sounds like a traditional triumphant prolongation of the tonic following a series of tonal cadences. Timpani and basses reiterate F–C motion, trumpet fanfares outline the tonic triad, and the music builds to a fortissimo dynamic level before a final upward thrust in octaves ends in a *fff* tutti F-major chord. In short, it *sounds* like coda music. Its similarity to other codas we have experienced helps us to accept it as a fitting close to the movement. Such similarity is important, for although an implied V_7–I progression in measures 873–75 reinforces the sense of closure at that point, there is no tonal harmonic closure just preceding the coda. Instead, the coda follows an unusual G♭–G–F progression of major triads in measures 865–67. The traditional cadential signs of a trill (in the woodwinds, brass, and percussion) and crescendo (in the E♭ clarinet, percussion, and strings) in measure 866 help to make the G-major triad sound like the penultimate harmony in a cadential progression. Thus Mahler creates final closure in the movement by using the conventional signs, but not the substance, of strong tonal harmonic closure.

Conclusive cadential progressions in the tonic are generally avoided in the third movement of Symphony No. 3, and final closure is accomplished without decisive tonal harmonic closure. A iii–♭II–I progression in measures 541–57 is followed by an extended tonic in a closing passage that is shaped by secondary parameters. The absence of motion in the primary parameters in measures 584–89 concentrates attention on the great intensifications in duration and dynamics. A gradual diminution of durations in measures 584–88 culminates in a trill that implies that durational closure will arrive when the trill ends. (After all, further durational diminution is not

EXAMPLE 4.36. Mahler, Symphony No. 9, IV, mm. 81–84.

possible.) A tremendous crescendo beginning in measure 584 also suggests closure is imminent, and the *fff* eighth-note chord in measure 590 produces durational and dynamic closure. The *fff* chord in measure 590 is the loudest in the movement. Thus, measures 584–90 provide an illustration of a relatively rare occurrence: extremely loud, final closure produced by processes in secondary parameters rather than cadential closure.

EXAMPLE 4.37. Mahler, Symphony No. 9, III, mm. 478–81.

In various movements and individual works Mahler uses a particular strategy for closure. In many of his songs, for example, there is a poetic and musical refrain that ends each strophe, as "Dunkel ist das Leben, ist der Tod" does in measures 81–89, 183–202, and 385–93 in the opening movement of *Das Lied von der Erde*.[55] Individual instrumental movements can have a special closing gesture as well. In the middle (C) section in the *Rondo-Burleske* of Symphony No. 9, for instance, the composer frequently articulates formal subdivisions with an ascending glissando or scale pattern leading to a soft, high-pitched tremolo in the violins. Example 4.37 illustrates the gesture, which, in addition to measures 479–81, occurs in measures 371–72, 391–92, 441–43, 447–49, 457–59, and 468–69. The gesture is another way in which Mahler "wipes the slate clean," so to speak. In each case durational closure, as occurs in measure 480 of Example 4.37, is strengthened by an increase in concordance in the same measure. Thus, the gesture is a sign of closure. On the other hand, from the start of the third section in measure 347 the violin tremolo is used as a ground for one or more figures in other parts, and consequently the tremolo is a sign of

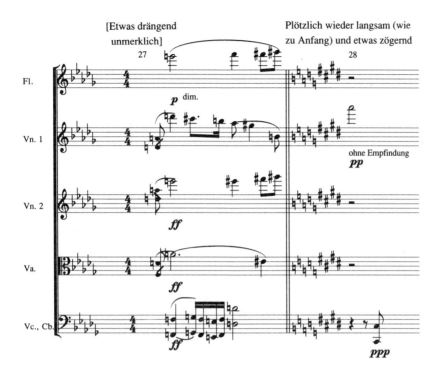

EXAMPLE 4.38. Mahler, Symphony No. 9, IV, mm. 27–28.

a beginning. There is a sense of elision, then, with regard to this gesture: it articulates both the end of a passage and the beginning of the next.

Many articulations in the last movement of Symphony No. 9 are created by a sudden reduction to a single pitch (or, on occasion, an octave) that is played softly and extended long enough to create durational closure. That sort of articulation is illustrated in Example 4.38, in which the abrupt reduction in components, sudden increase in concordance, and durational closure in measure 28 mark both the end of the first primary thematic section of the movement and the beginning of the second (C♯-minor) thematic section. The sudden change in components and dynamics calls attention to the single pitch A6 in the first violins as the beginning of a passage. At the same time, the A6 clearly follows from the ascending pitch pattern in the flutes and second violins in measure 27, and because of its length there is simple and compound durational closure in measure 28. The durational closure indicates the conclusion of the primary thematic section. Conformant articulations occur in measures 11, 32, 38, 88, 92, and 101, where the gesture also signals both a conclusion and a beginning.

Finally, as we conclude this examination of compositional strategies for closure using secondary parameters, consider the use of repeated gestures of abating closure to conclude high-level hierarchic structures. Repeated tonal cadences are a common means of signifying the end of a large section or movement, and repeated abating closure can serve the same function. In Mahler's music such abating closure typically includes at least one gesture of subsidence. Recall that particularly convincing closure is created by the combined effects of sinking to the bottom, on the one hand, and growing more tranquil and quiet, on the other hand. A final example of subsidence incorporates both effects (Example 4.39).

Though the primary parameters are most important for creating closure in the last movement of the Sixth Symphony, secondary parameters are primarily responsible for final, ultimate, closure. The fact that measures 773 and following conform to the very opening of the movement creates a sense of balance and symmetry, and

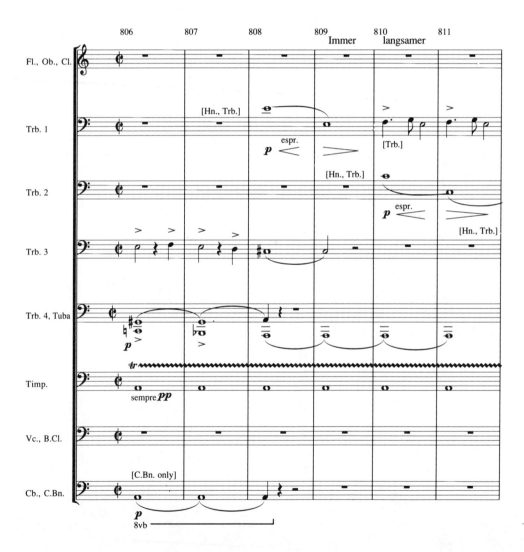

EXAMPLE 4.39. Mahler, Symphony No. 6, IV, mm. 806–22.

suggests that final closure is pending. After the discordant $V^7_{5\flat}$ harmony in measure 807 resolves to the tonic in measure 808, three different closing gestures (in measures 808–16, 816–19, and 820–22) bring the movement to a close.

The descending octaves in the horns and trombones in measures 808–16 (E4–E3, C4–C3, A3–A2) lead down through the tonic triad and create the effect of settling to the bottom. Abating durations support the closing gesture in measures 809–16 while contributing to a sense of growing tranquility. (Notice the indication "immer langsamer" at measure 809.) In particular, the durational pattern of the first two descending octaves is augmented in measures 812–16. Moreover, the durational

EXAMPLE 4.39 (cont.)

pattern in the first trombone at measure 810 (second staff down) is augmented in measures 812–16. The timpani sustains an A2 pedal throughout measures 790–818, so the completion of the descending octave pattern on A2 in measure 814 creates strong registral pitch closure. A dynamic abatement in measures 814–16 is terminally synchronized with durational closure in the trombone part at measure 816.

The second closing gesture begins in measure 816 like the introduction in measure 16.[56] The ♩ ♪ ♫ ♩ motive in the bassoon and basses at measure 817 is

EXAMPLE 4.39 (*cont.*)

augmented in measures 818–19, just as the conformant motive ♩. ♪ ♩ was augmented in the first trombone part at measures 812–16. Because of conformant patterning, there is registral pitch closure in the second half of measure 818, in addition to component and concordant closure. Fading dynamics strengthen the impression that the passage will fade to silence, filling us with a sense of tranquility. Final closure seems imminent.

There is no need to point out to anyone who has heard the final measures of the symphony, and in particular any listener familiar with Mahler's style, that the overall effect of these first two abating gestures is entirely convincing; no doubt the startling, dramatic, even terrifying *ff* crash of measure 820 is indelibly etched in memory. The absence of the anticipated silence makes the fortissimo statement of the symphony's motto especially forceful.[57] Although there is no descending pitch pattern in any individual part in measures 820–22, as parts drop out there is a kind of composed descent in pitch from the C6/A5 of the woodwinds in measure 820 to the triad on A4 in the trumpets in measures 820–21 to the final pizzicato A1/A2/A3 in the strings at measure 822. The most important abatements, of course, are in simple and compound dynamics, which are dramatically reduced in measures 820–21. Decreasing components contribute to the diminishing compound dynamic level, which once again approaches silence. The final string pizzicato in measure 822 articulates the end of the diminuendo, and thereby the end of the movement and the symphony.

Taken as a whole, Example 4.39 presents all the classic signs of subsiding closure: descending pitch patterns falling to a sustained pedal, decreasing components, augmented durations, and diminishing dynamics.

*   *   *

It is clear that in Mahler's music secondary parameters often play a crucial role in defining closure, though that role varies considerably from movement to movement and work to work, and the precise ways in which secondary parameters produce closure are remarkably varied. In certain movements Mahler employs a specially characteristic method of shaping form or creating closure. In many works Mahler skillfully adapts a basic compositional strategy—be it collapse, fragmentation, subsidence, or some other strategy—to the specific musical context. Having considered individual examples of Mahler's use of secondary parameters to articulate musical form, we now turn to an overall view of the use and importance of secondary parameters for creating closure in his works.

CHAPTER 5

Closing Observations

In this chapter we will discuss trends in Mahler's use of abating closure, examine the relative importance of primary and secondary parameters for creating closure in the composer's works, and assess the significance of the composer's strategies for articulating musical form.

As we have seen, Mahler most often used abatements in duration or in components to create abating closure, especially in the symphonic works. When two or more different kinds of secondary parameters lead to closure at more or less the same time, one of the parameters is almost always duration.[1] For example, durational and concordant closure occur on the downbeat of measure 22 in Example 4.35. If at least three different kinds of secondary parameters create closure at essentially the same time—a relatively unusual occurrence—two of them are typically duration and components. For instance, concordant closure together with durational and component closure creates repose at the beginning of measure 73 in Example 4.9. Durational and component closure is generally enhanced by abatements in dynamics, registral pitch, and concordance.

Almost every time that processes in duration and *concordance* create closure, the repose is supported by abatements in registral pitch, dynamics, and components (and sometimes by registral pitch or component closure). See Example 4.35. Such durational and concordant closure is typically used to conclude a section within a movement. In contrast, abatements leading to durational and *dynamic* closure usually occur at the end of a movement.

It may be that durational/dynamic closure occurs far less frequently in the midst of a movement or song because Mahler was concerned to write continuous music; dynamic closure resulting from fading dynamics does not allow the possibility for continuation by any means other than elision. That is, one can have component closure and still have continuing motion in the remaining component, and likewise one can have concordant closure or registral pitch closure and still have forward motion as a result of some intensifying process in one or more components. When durations fade to silence or to the softest possible dynamic level, however, any sense of forward motion tends to disappear with the sound.

Apparently for Mahler durational/dynamic closure was particularly appropriate and effective for ending slow movements and slow songs. He consistently uses such closure to conclude slow pieces, including the slowest movement in each symphony except for the Eighth and Tenth Symphonies.[2] The only slow movements that do not conclude with durational/dynamic closure are the Finale of the Third Symphony and the first movement of the Tenth.[3] Usually the durational/dynamic closure concludes a tonic prolongation following strong syntactic closure. Only at the end of Symphony No. 4, IV (Example 4.26) does another secondary parameter, namely components, create closure in addition to duration and dynamics.

Durational and dynamic closure rarely combine to conclude a subsection in a movement except in the last movement of *Das Lied von der Erde* and in Symphony No. 2, in which dynamic closure occurs about twice as often as in any other symphony. (See Example 4.27.) The durational/dynamic closure just before the coda in the third movement of the Fifth Symphony (Example 4.21) is a notable exception.[4]

Of all the secondary parameters, concordance is probably the least influential in shaping the ends of passages, even though concordant closure occurs about as often as registral pitch closure and, except in the vocal works, far more often than dynamic closure. Concordance is a contributing force but generally not decisive with respect to the articulation of form because abatements in concordance are quite brief and somewhat less apparent than abatements in dynamics, registral pitch, or components. There are at least two reasons for this. One is that tonality is a powerful force in Mahler's music, and harmonies are typically organized according to stylistic rules rather than strategies of increasing (or decreasing) concordance. A second reason is that much of Mahler's music is contrapuntally conceived; as a result, processes of strictly increasing concordance lasting more than a few beats are rather unlikely. Many times a reduction in components produces an increase in concordance (as in Example 4.30), and it is the reduction in components that is more striking.

Dynamic closure occurs only about half as often as concordant, registral pitch, or component closure in the symphonies. However, dynamics are probably the most widely used secondary parameter for *enhancing* abating closure and articulating musical form. As we saw in the last chapter, abatements in dynamics are often coupled with abatements in registral pitch to produce gestures of subsidence. Subsiding passages are generally used in the symphonies to articulate the end of a primary or secondary thematic section. Subsiding passages following a dynamic climax occur in every symphony.[5]

One of the important points about subsiding passages is that they articulate the conclusion of one passage while at the same time providing a transition—be it harmonic, dynamic, registral, or durational—to the next section. The subsiding passage in Example 4.28, for instance, leads from the extremely loud, high-pitched climax of measure 210 to the varied return of the pianissimo first theme in its original, moderately low register at measure 222. In addition, there is a transition from the F♯ minor of measures 210–15 to G major in measure 222.

In general, dissolutions shape the end of one passage while providing some sort of transition to the next. In Example 4.11 the dissolution of the A-minor sonority in measures 94–97 ends with a solo oboe playing C, the common tone in a direct modulation from the A minor of the scherzo to the F major of the trio. Moreover, the lengthening of the basic pulse (an eighth-note duration) in measures 92–97 provides a durational transition to the slower trio section that follows.

In Mahler's works, then, by far the most common closure produced by secondary parameters is durational closure, so simple and compound duration are the most important secondary parameters for articulating form. Components are the next most important articulating force. Reductions in components are frequently accompanied by decreasing dynamics and generally increasing concordance. Abating components are a vital part of processes of dissolution. Concordance, on the other hand, is probably the least influential secondary parameter next to timbre; indeed, there are few continuous, straightforward processes of increasing concordance. Often concordant closure is basically a consequence of component closure. Registral pitch and dynamics are of approximately equal importance. Registral pitch closure is only slightly less frequent than component closure, and abatements in registral pitch are crucial in defining many gestures of subsidence. Dynamic closure is relatively rare in the later symphonies, but rather common in the vocal works, and decreasing dynamics are an influential shaping force in most abatements. On many occasions diminishing dynamics play a crucial role in creating subsidence after a dynamic climax. Many songs conclude with dynamic closure.

*   *   *

How important are secondary parameters compared to primary parameters for creating closure in Mahler's works? There is no simple answer, especially since Mahler's use of primary and secondary parameters to articulate conclusions can vary significantly from one work—and sometimes from one movement—to the next. The symphonies may be taken as representative of the varying importance of primary and secondary parameters in Mahler's music, and though the conclusions we reach in this chapter are based on an examination of the vocal works as well as the symphonies, we will focus attention on the evidence from the symphonies.

The First Symphony probably has the most diatonic harmony of all the symphonies, and processes in tonal pitch and harmony define the most important points of closure. In several passages, however, the use of extended pedal tones weakens the closural force of cadences. As a result, secondary parameters play a significant role in articulating formal divisions.[6] Tonic prolongations following cadential closure are generally ended by abatements in secondary parameters. The parameters of registral pitch, components, and dynamics are especially influential.

Abating closure is more frequent in Symphony No. 2 than in Symphony No. 1, chiefly because abatements in dynamics and components lead to closure more often.

Subsiding gestures are particularly important for creating closure and shaping the ends of passages when traditional tonal cadences are not a decisive organizing force: as in the trio sections of the second movement, in the third movement, and in the first part of the fifth movement.[7] On the other hand, primary parameters are crucial, and secondary parameters relatively unimportant, for creating closure in the fourth movement and the last part of the fifth (measures 448–764) where vocal resources are employed.[8]

In the Third Symphony, secondary parameters play a major role in articulating form in the first and fourth movements, especially where tonal harmony is static.[9] As in the Second Symphony, the secondary parameters are generally most important for creating closure in those movements where traditional tonal cadences are not common,[10] although abating closure does mark the ends of three large sections in the Finale.[11] Primary parameters are particularly important for articulating form in the second, fifth, and sixth movements.

Except for Symphony No. 1, the Fourth Symphony may have the most diatonic melodies and harmonies of all the symphonies, and, not surprisingly, traditional tonal cadences commonly create closure. The last two movements are rather unusual in that both cadential and abating processes are prominently used to produce closure at the ends of major sections.[12]

In Symphony No. 5 there is more frequent use of chromatic, discordant counterpoint. Secondary parameters play a vital role in articulating closure in the first two movements of the symphony,[13] and a far less important role in the last three movements, where very diatonic themes and strong syntactic processes are more common. Many formal divisions in the second, third, and fifth movements are articulated by the start of a section rather than the close of one.

Strong closure is rare in the first movement of Symphony No. 6, and here, too, most of the time the end of a closing passage is only articulated by the beginning of the next. Overall, tonal harmony is probably less important for creating closure than in any of the first five symphonies. Save for the Finale, syntactic processes are an important organizing force only in parts of the second movement. Secondary parameters are decisive in articulating form in the Scherzo.[14]

Deryck Cooke has said that the first movement of the Seventh Symphony "carries further the tonal disruption of the Sixth: the superimposed fourths, bitonality, and violent key-switches from bar to bar, introduced new elements into the language of modern music."[15] This observation suggests that secondary parameters might play an important role in articulating sections in the movement—and that is the case. Strong abating closure, however, does not occur often. Abating processes may indicate that a passage is coming to a close, but frequently the end of the passage is articulated by the beginning of the next section rather than by abating closure. Secondary parameters are crucial in defining closure throughout the second movement; abating processes shape the end of the introduction as well as each part of the rondo form.[16] Secondary parameters are very important in articulating formal divisions in the third movement as well (see Example 4.13), but the lack of strong durational closure weakens many points of repose.[17] As in the Sixth Symphony, secondary parameters are weakest as an organizing force in the Finale (where, unlike the Finale of No. 6, strong closure of any sort is relatively uncommon).

Substantial abating closure is rare in the Eighth Symphony, and in fact secondary parameters play a very limited role in articulating formal divisions. There are frequent and usually emphatic instances of cadential closure throughout the symphony, but they are followed by relatively few tonic prolongations that might be closed by abating processes. Many points of syntactic closure are elided with the beginnings of other passages.[18] Moreover, Mahler has less need for secondary parameters to shape musical form because textual closure and abrupt changes in the number and kinds of voices help to articulate the form.

There are few points of strong closure in the opening and closing movements of Symphony No. 9. The third movement is a *Rondo-Burleske,* and, like several other rondos by Mahler, its formal divisions are most often articulated by the beginnings— rather than the conclusions—of phrases and sections.[19] As in the fast third movements of Symphony Nos. 6 and 7, the third movement is notable for the relative scarcity of traditional tonal cadences. Like the slower inner movements of Symphony Nos. 5–7 (that is: No. 5, IV; No. 6, II; and No. 7, IV), the second movement of Symphony No. 9 is marked by frequent strong syntactic closure; abating closure is relatively rare.

Abating processes are important for shaping form in the first movement of the Tenth Symphony, but there are few points of overall closure.[20]

Overall, the primary parameters are very important for articulating closure in the first four symphonies as well as in the Eighth Symphony, which may be considered "a throwback to the Mahler of Symphonies 2, 3, and 4."[21] Cadential closure is generally crucial for producing repose in those movements that include one or more vocal parts: that is, Symphony No. 2, IV and V; Symphony No. 3, IV and V; Symphony No. 4, IV; and all of Symphony No. 8.[22] The primary parameters are most important for creating closure in Symphony Nos. 1, 4, and 8, which on the whole are characterized by thematic statements employing the most diatonic themes and harmonies in the symphonies. On the other hand, cadential closure is distinctly less influential in producing closure in Symphony Nos. 5, 6, 7, 9, and 10, which include more chromatic themes and harmonies than the other works. There is general agreement that these later symphonies are symptomatic of the gradual attenuation of tonal syntax during the early part of the twentieth century. In general, strong cadential closure is most common in the slow movements and finales of these symphonies (as it is, also, in Symphony Nos. 2 and 3), and least important in the first movements and fast or moderately fast inner movements.

Turning now to Mahler's use of secondary parameters for articulating musical form and particularly for creating, not just supporting, closure: we see that abating closure is least common in the First and Eighth Symphonies and most common in the Fifth Symphony. In order to appreciate the full significance of abating closure, though, one must consider the specific context. There are many examples of abating closure in the Fourth Symphony, for instance, but most of them (like the passage given in Example 4.35) come just after, or together with, strong cadential closure. Such instances of abating repose, while noteworthy, must be considered less significant than those instances (like the passage given in Example 4.6) in which secondary parameters alone are primarily responsible for concluding a passage.[23] Often when secondary parameters are chiefly responsible for closure, the repose is also supported by tonal pitch closure (as in Example 4.25).

Another important consideration is Mahler's tendency to avoid strong closure, whether cadential or abating, in many movements of Symphony Nos. 5, 6, 7, 9, and 10. His apparent desire for a more continuous flow of music is reflected most clearly in Symphony No. 9 and the first movement of No. 10. There are fewer instances of substantial abating closure in the Ninth Symphony than in the Fourth Symphony, but because of the relative scarcity of weighty closure in Symphony No. 9 the few instances of strong abating closure in the symphony take on added significance. Moreover, there is a growing tendency in the later symphonies (except for No. 8) for Mahler to use abrupt changes in secondary parameters to articulate the beginnings of passages. That is particularly true in the Ninth Symphony (except for the second movement) and the first movement of the Tenth.[24] Other movements in which secondary parameters play a prominent role in articulating the beginnings of passages include Symphony No. 5, II and III; No. 6, I; and No. 7, I and V.[25]

Generally speaking, secondary parameters are most important for creating closure and otherwise articulating musical form in movements where significant cadential closure is least common. Such movements typically include first movements and fast or moderately fast inner movements: Symphony No. 2, III; No. 3, I; No. 4, III; No. 5, I, II, and III; No. 6, III; No. 7, I and III; No. 9, III; and No. 10, I.[26] Secondary parameters are also a powerful organizing force in the first, exclusively instrumental part (measures 1–447) of Symphony No. 2, V, where strong cadential closure is rare. The third movements of Symphony Nos. 6 and 9 are extreme cases; secondary parameters are crucial for articulating form throughout the movements, which do not include any strong authentic cadence in the tonic. In contrast, the third movement of Symphony No. 4 is unusual because it is a movement in which both primary and secondary parameters are very important for articulating the form.

Secondary parameters generally play a less important role in movements incorporating one or more vocal parts (that is: Symphony No. 2, IV and V; No. 3, IV and V; No. 4, IV; and No. 8, both I and II). There may be less need for secondary parameters to articulate form in movements where the structure of the text can influence closure, and formal articulations can be easily produced by changes in the number and kinds of voices or by rests in the vocal part(s).

Abating closure is probably least influential in articulating form in the two choral movements of the Eighth Symphony. Unlike other symphonies in which primary parameters are a decisive organizing force, the Eighth Symphony includes relatively few tonic prolongations following cadential closure. In other symphonies, such tonic prolongations are typically closed, or at least shaped, by abating processes in secondary parameters. In the First Symphony, for example, when abating closure occurs it often concludes a tonic prolongation following strong cadential closure (as in Examples 4.7 and 4.14). Nevertheless, there are few examples of abating closure in the First Symphony, and only rarely are secondary parameters chiefly responsible for closure. (Examples 4.6 and 4.16 are unusual in that respect.) The same is true of the Third Symphony, except for the first movement. Thus, secondary parameters are least important for articulating musical form in Symphony Nos. 1, 3, and 8. It is not coincidental that these are symphonies in which primary parameters are especially influential in creating closure.

Overall, secondary parameters tend to be less prominent in shaping form in the slow movements and finales, where primary parameters tend to be decisive in articulating the form. One reason why secondary parameters generally have less impact on the articulation of form in the slow movements may have to do with the basic texture of most of the slow movements. It seems reasonable to expect that tonality would be a stronger organizing force in movements where the predominant texture is homophonic, rather than polyphonic. That is so because, in general, a homophonic texture draws attention to the vertical (chordal) aspect of the music, whereas a polyphonic texture draws attention to the horizontal (linear) aspect of the music. Furthermore, subsidence after a loud climax is a common means of abating closure, but dynamics are a less effective shaping force in many slow movements where, on the whole, loud dynamic levels are unusual. That is because the dynamic range in many slow movements is relatively restricted. (See, for instance, Symphony No. 1, III; No. 2, IV; and No. 3, IV.)

Secondary parameters generally play a minor role in creating closure in finales, which typically include very diatonic thematic material. Not surprisingly, primary parameters are usually decisive in articulating the form. In fact, most symphonies conclude with a rather traditional, fortissimo extension of the tonic following repeated syntactic closure. (See the conclusions of Symphony Nos. 1, 2, 3, 5, 7, and 8.) The Finale of Symphony No. 9 is a notable exception. Primary parameters are probably less important than secondary parameters for articulating the form in that movement, which includes far more chromatic thematic material than most other finales. Durational and dynamic closure bring the movement to a final conclusion (Example 4.12). The Finales of Symphony Nos. 4 and 6 also end quietly.

How important are secondary parameters compared to primary parameters for articulating form in Mahler's works? Based on an examination of the symphonies as well as the songs, primary parameters are more important on the whole, which is to be expected in works that are considered part of the repertory of tonal music. Nevertheless, an examination of Mahler's works, including the songs, reveals that secondary parameters—in particular durations, components, and dynamics—are a very influential shaping force.

Ample evidence indicates that, in general, secondary parameters are strongest as an organizing force in those works where primary parameters are least influential for articulating form, and secondary parameters are weakest in movements where primary parameters are strongest. Thus, the decline of tonal syntax in Mahler's works is matched by a concomitant increase in the importance of secondary parameters for articulating musical form. The fact that tonic prolongations following strong cadential closure are often shaped or concluded by abating secondary parameters reinforces the view that abating closure is most influential when primary parameters are least important—in this case, when the primary parameters are essentially static. Further studies of works by Mahler's contemporaries are needed so we can learn the extent to which composers of the late nineteenth and early twentieth centuries used secondary parameters to compensate for the weakening of tonality as an organizing force.

*   *   *

In this book we have concentrated our attention on examples that illustrate higher-level structural closure as opposed to closure only on the level of the individual phrase because our chief interest is in how Mahler compensated for the lack of cadential closure in his works. The composer's growing tendency throughout his life to avoid strong tonal harmonic closure in his works (again, except for Symphony No. 8), and to rely instead upon secondary parameters for articulating musical form, was a contributing factor in the decline of tonality since the cadence is, after all, a central feature of tonality and the way in which it is confirmed. At the same time, though, Mahler's use of abating closure opened up new possibilities for more continuous, yet clearly articulated, music.

In a remarkable number of interesting ways, Mahler employed gestures of dissolution as significant signs of closure. These passages help prepare the listener not only for a conclusion but also, in a broader and very important sense, for the beginning of the next passage. Even when an overall abatement in several secondary parameters does not lead to a specific, implied point of closure, the closing function of the passage is usually clear and the listener is ready for the beginning of another passage. Unlike a full authentic cadence, in which the penultimate dominant is tensive, an overall abatement in secondary parameters grows increasingly more restful. Even if it fails to reach an implied point of conclusion, the abatement still ends on a point of relative repose.

Mahler's use of abating closure contributed to the composition of music that is contrapuntally conceived and often lacking in strong tonal harmonic cadences. Secondary parametric processes are especially well suited to shaping form in a contrapuntal texture that, to repeat Michael Kennedy's words, "became detached from the conventional sense of tonality, with each part independent of the other and liable to separate development."[27] Mahler needed ways of indicating closure while maintaining the contrapuntal fabric, and as we have seen in many examples, dissolutions can effectively shape the end of one passage while at the same time providing a transition to the next—and do it in a way that audiences can easily follow. There is a clear trend in Mahler's works toward composing music that has very few overall strong points of closure, but is characterized by clearly-differentiated structures based on shaping processes in secondary parameters and distinctly-articulated beginnings generally created by an abrupt change in one or more secondary parameters.

One of the crucial shaping processes in Mahler's music is a subsiding gesture in which the music fades away. Frequent use of such subsidence had a significant impact on the overall shape of his musical compositions. By letting the music fade to a soft dynamic level, Mahler allowed the possibility of building up to a climax that could then be followed by subsidence, another (bigger) climax, and so on, a procedure that is well-known to students of nineteenth- and early twentieth-century music.[28] Leonard Ratner writes that "a great many compositions of this era fail to arrive emphatically; they trail off, leaving a question unanswered."[29] Exactly what Ratner had in mind is unclear, but the statement prompts me to make this one last point. Final closure created by secondary parameters is different in character from emphatic cadential closure, but it is no less final because it is not emphatic. Indeed, such closure is generally more indicative of rest and repose than emphatic, cadential closure.

> This is the way the world ends
> This is the way the world ends
> This is the way the world ends
>   Not with a bang, but a whimper.*

*Excerpt from "The Hollow Men" from *Collected Poems 1909–1962* By T. S. Eliot, copyright 1936 by Harcourt Brace Jovanovich, Inc. and copyright 1964, 1963 by T. S. Eliot; reprinted by permission of the publisher.

NOTES

Chapter 1: Introduction

1. The term *parameter* may be defined as a variable in a musical expression, each value of which restricts or determines the specific form and substance of the expression. This definition is adapted from *The American Heritage Dictionary of the English Language,* s.v. "parameter." *Parameter* is used in two senses throughout this book: (1) to refer to one of the several parameters *of* music, and (2) to refer to the elements—that is, the values—of a particular parameter *in* music. For a more detailed discussion of the use of the term parameter, see chapter 3.

2. For a detailed discussion of how primary parameters are distinguished from secondary parameters, see chapter 2. In this study I shall consider rhythm to be a summarizing parameter, a result of the interaction of grouping and metrical structures; see Fred Lerdahl and Ray Jackendoff, *A New Generative Theory of Tonal Music* (Cambridge, Mass: MIT Press, 1983), 12–104. By durations, on the other hand, I mean simply the actual lengths in time of notes and rests. Thus, durational differences can create rhythmic structures, but in music rhythmic structures are a result of the interaction of all parameters: "To study rhythm is to study all of music. Rhythm both organizes, and is itself organized by, all the elements which create and shape musical processes." (Grosvenor W. Cooper and Leonard B. Meyer, *The Rhythmic Structure of Music* [Chicago: University of Chicago Press, 1960], 1.)

3. Eugene Narmour, "Some Major Theoretical Problems Concerning the Concept of Hierarchy in the Analysis of Tonal Music," *Music Perception* 1 (Winter 1983–84): 156. Narmour also discusses closural and nonclosural aspects of music in his book *Beyond Schenkerism: The Need for Alternatives in Music Analysis* (Chicago: University of Chicago Press, 1977), 98–107.

4. *The New Harvard Dictionary of Music,* s.v. "cadence."

5. Ibid.

Chapter 2: Closure

1. This definition, and the discussion that follows, owes much to the work of Barbara Herrnstein Smith. See Smith, *Poetic Closure: A Study of How Poems End* (Chicago: University of Chicago Press, 1968).

2. The distinction between closure in a particular parameter (independent of the actual musical context) and overall closure is discussed below.

3. The word *element* will be used to describe a value for a parameter. Middle C, for example, can be an element of pitch, and an E-major triad an element of harmony.

4. As Leonard B. Meyer has stated: "Our sense of completeness is directly related to our ability to understand the meaning of a particular pattern. A stimulus series which develops no process, awakens no tendencies, will . . . always appear to be incomplete." See Meyer, *Emotion and Meaning in Music* (Chicago: University of Chicago Press, 1956), 138–39.

5. Accordingly, in this study the words *conclude* and *finish* will be used as synonyms for *close*. Something that ends, however, may close, or may merely stop (terminate, cease).

6. Smith, *Poetic Closure*, 2. According to Hans and Shulamith Kreitler, "Evocation of pleasure . . . is concomitant with a rise in tension followed by a reduction in tension." See *Psychology of the Arts* (Durham, N.C.: Duke University Press, 1972), 13.

7. This discussion relies upon the work of Wallace Berry, who discusses motion, both directed and undirected, on pages 4–9 of his book *Structural Functions in Music* (Englewood Cliffs, N.J.: Prentice-Hall, 1970).

8. The terms *intensifying* and *abating* correspond to *progressive* and *recessive,* respectively, in Berry, *Structural Functions in Music,* 7.

9. This term is borrowed from Leonard B. Meyer. See *Explaining Music: Essays and Explorations* (Berkeley: University of California Press, 1973), 81.

10. Registral pitch is a secondary parameter that refers to pitch without regard to tonal function or significance. It is differentiated from the primary parameter of tonal pitch in the next chapter.

11. Timbre is a notable exception. See chapter 3.

12. The increase in tension can actually be a pleasurable experience, because we can anticipate the pleasure of an imminent resolution. See Hans and Shulamith Kreitler, *Psychology of the Arts,* 13–16. It may well be that one reason we find it "natural" to want to slow down at an ending is that it increases our pleasure with the conclusion by creating a small rise in tension prior to the achievement of closure.

13. To articulate is to mark distinctly. Basically, one can articulate the end of a musical passage either by bringing it to a conclusion or by beginning another passage. Thus, an articulation can be a point of arrival or a point of departure, or both.

14. See Meyer, *Emotion and Meaning,* 128–29.

15. Of course some twentieth-century works do not exhibit hierarchic structure. Others that do often rely upon pitch manipulations that are difficult for many listeners to detect. Mahler among others was able to use patterns and processes in secondary parameters to build and clarify hierarchic structures in his music, including pieces that eschewed traditional authentic and plagal cadences. Listeners' abilities to perceive the patterns and processes in secondary parameters may account in part for the continued popularity of Mahler's music today.

16. Although the first statement of a small-scale event may not actually be closed, the repetition of that event (varied or not) creates the expectation that it will end in a similar manner and, accordingly, the repetition may be closed.

17. This is not to deny that closure is relative, of course, and that some passages are more closed than others.

18. Smith, *Poetic Closure,* 36.

19. Ibid., 213.

20. Secondary parametric closure, the subject of chapter 3, can be an exception.

21. The term *conformant* is taken from Leonard Meyer, who discusses conformant relationships at length in chapter 3 of *Explaining Music.*

22. Return must be differentiated from mere repetition. Return is the repetition of an event after some contrasting event. See Meyer, *Emotion and Meaning,* 151–53.

23. Keep in mind that we are only talking about formal events here, not processes. Often, of course, A' does not end exactly like A because a process left incomplete in A is completed in A'. With reference to the principle of return, the differences are important only to the extent that A' becomes so different from A as to weaken the sense of return.

24. See Kurt Koffka, *Principles of Gestalt Psychology* (New York: Harcourt, Brace & Co., 1935), 110.

25. This statement in no way denies that processive relationships between A′ and previous sections can help create closure at the end of A′. Often, for example, the closure of A′ is strong because it completes a process begun in B.

26. This is especially true because such a series of cadences is a conventional closing gesture in tonal music.

27. To put it another way, how do we know which cadence will be the last? If there is no implied termination, the last cadence may be heard as a stop rather than a close.

28. The strength of the conformant relationship will also be influenced by how well the gesture is ingrained in the mind of the listener. Nothing prevents a composer from using the same gesture several times in a single work, of course. Schumann employs the closing gesture shown in Example 2.8 (three tonic chords) at the conclusion of the first, third, and fourth movements of his Piano Sonata No. 3 in F Minor, op. 14. Ordinarily, though, a listener compares his or her current experience of a gesture with the memory of a similar event heard at a different time and, perhaps, in a different place.

29. Example 2.7b is not as closed as 2.7a and 2.7c since the tonic in measure 42 is left immediately. A series of authentic cadences follows in measures 42–50.

30. When only the third chord is followed by a rest (as in Example 2.8a and 2.8c) the listener will perceive the third chord as being longer than the previous two, so that durational closure is created. Durational closure will also occur if the performers hold the final chord slightly longer than the preceding two. Such closure is discussed in chapter 3.

31. The terminology used to describe cadences lacks uniformity. In this study, *perfect authentic cadence* refers to a harmonic progression that marks the end of a phrase, section, or movement and either consists of or ends with $V_{(7)}$–I, where both chords are in root position and the tonic is in the top voice of the tonic triad. Often a series of perfect authentic cadences is used to create closure at the ends of major sections or the conclusion of the movement (or work).

32. The need for such conventional ending signals is discussed below.

33. Peter W. Culicover, *Syntax* (New York: Academic Press, 1976), 4.

34. Edward Cone has made the same point with respect to musical gestures: "Like a sigh, a musical gesture has no specific referent, it conveys no specific message. But like a sigh it can prove appropriate to many occasions; it can fit into many contexts, which in return can explain its significance. The expressive content of the musical gesture, then, depends on its context. Deprived of context, the gesture expresses nothing; it is only potentially expressive." Edward T. Cone, *The Composer's Voice* (Berkeley: University of California Press, 1974), 165. Even when our experience leads us to believe that a particular musical element will be used in a certain way, we cannot be assured that it will not act in any of several different ways. For example, the sound created by G–B–D–F usually functions as the dominant of a chord whose root is C. However, the sound might function as a subdominant if it is resolved in the manner of an augmented six-five-three chord.

35. Of course, music can still be ungrammatical.

36. My discussion of syntax owes much to Leonard B. Meyer's treatment of the topic in "Toward a Theory of Style," in *The Concept of Style,* ed. Berel Lang (Philadelphia: University of Pennsylvania Press, 1979), 18–27. One important difference is that Meyer includes rhythm as a syntactic parameter.

37. In the Baroque period, dynamics satisfied the requirement.

38. We can discriminate variations of about three cycles per second at frequencies up to approximately 1000 cycles per second. At 1000 cycles per second, then, we can hear a difference of 1/20th of a half step. At frequencies above 1000 cycles per second, we can hear changes equal to 1/25th of a half step. See John Backus, *The Acoustical Foundations of Music* (New York: W. W. Norton, 1969), 113.

39. This recognition, of course, depends upon an accepted standard of pitch, such as A = 440. (There is no equivalent standard of duration.) For many, the sense of pitch is defined well enough to judge consistently whether a performer is playing a pitch accurately, or sharp or flat.

40. The word *interval* is used here to mean "the extent of difference between two qualities, conditions, etc." *Webster's New Twentieth Century Dictionary of the English Language,* 2d ed., s.v. "interval."

41. In retrospect, of course, we realize that the crescendo ended at a certain point, but that does not mean it is closed retrospectively. As we argued above, closing should be differentiated from stopping. The end of the crescendo is not articulated by closure, but by the beginning of another dynamic process or pattern. Closure, retrospective or not, occurs only when relative repose is realized at a point implied by one or more parametric processes or patterns.

42. This does not deny that there are points of closure in a series of abating durations, but there is no internal basis for deciding which duration will close an abating pattern. Durational closure is discussed in chapter 3.

43. Registral pitch and concordance will refer to those psychological aspects of frequencies that are completely independent of tonality, and tonal pitch and harmony will refer to the tonal aspects.

44. Of these processive relationships, only an abating series can lead to closure. Processes of that sort are discussed in chapter 3.

45. The reader will recall that in this study rhythm is considered a summarizing primary parameter, and is differentiated from duration. Some readers may nevertheless object to grouping durations with the secondary parameters rather than with the primary, syntactic parameters of tonal pitch and harmony. This grouping does not in any way discount the importance of durational patterning in creating processive relationships. It does, however, acknowledge that there are no clear rules for ordering durations within a phrase, that generally speaking durational relationships are not dependent on style as are syntactic parameters, and that durations are distinctly secondary to melody and harmony in articulating form in tonal music. One might well consider: are the kinds of processes created by durations more like those created by tonal pitch and harmony, or more like those in other secondary parameters?

46. Even though the fifth degree is more stable than the third, there are more tonal cadences ending with the melody on the third degree. That is because descending stepwise motion is preferred at a cadence (see the discussion of registral pitch in chapter 3), and one cannot write a stepwise descent to the fifth degree when the underlying harmonies are V_7–I. Only when composers began using V_9–I progressions was stepwise descent to the fifth degree possible.

47. The term *consonant* is used to refer to elements that do not require resolution, and *dissonant* to refer to elements that require resolution, according to the rules of the style.

48. Walter Piston and Marc DeVoto, *Harmony,* 5th ed. (New York: W. W. Norton, 1987), 23.

49. It is interesting to study the use of the dominant seventh chord in the nineteenth century. Through repetition, the dominant seventh lost some of its impact as a tensive sound entity. Composers sought out alternative chords, such as the dominant seventh with augmented or diminished fifths, the dominant ninth, and the dominant thirteenth, all of which maintained a dominant function and provided a more dissonant and therefore tensive sound. For a discussion of how training and exposure can influence aesthetic preferences, see F. G. Hare, "Artistic Training and Response to Visual and Auditory Patterns Varying in Uncertainty," in *Studies in the New Experimental Aesthetics,* ed. D. E. Berlyne (New York: Halsted, 1974), 159–68.

50. Thus, what is considered complete and stable depends upon the listener's understanding of the overall musical context. A slow introduction to the first movement of a symphony may end on V and be complete and stable as an introduction, but harmonically it is incomplete so the closure at the end of the introduction would be relatively weak.

51. Of course a musical context can greatly alter the strength of a particular kind of cadence. The influence of secondary parameters on harmonic closure is discussed at length in chapter 3.

52. The completion of higher-level processes is subject to "the law of hierarchic equivalence: an event is an adequate realization of an implication only if it is on a hierarchic level which is the same as, or more extended than, the level of the pattern which generated the implications in question." Meyer, *Explaining Music,* 134.

53. According to Heinrich Schenker, total closure is created when the fundamental line and bass arpeggiation arrive at the tonic: "To man is given the experience of ending, the cessation of all tensions and efforts. In this sense, we feel by nature that the fundamental must lead downward until it reaches $\hat{1}$,

and that the bass must fall back to the fundamental. With $\hat{1}$ all tensions in a musical work cease." (*Free Composition* [*Der Freie Satz*], ed. and trans. Ernst Oster [New York: Longman, 1979], 13.) On the contrary, *all* tensions do not necessarily cease with the arrival of $\hat{1}$—only those created by the syntactic parameters. Moreover, one cannot assume that all tensions associated with the syntactic parameters will cease forever once the fundamental structure is completed. For instance, if the music that follows $\hat{1}$ departs from the tonic and musical elements are related to a different tonal center, tensions will arise that can be resolved only by a return to the tonic. Schenker's definition of closure does not allow for that possibility, however. "With the arrival of $\hat{1}$ [together with I] the work is at an end. Whatever follows this can only be a reinforcement of the close—a coda—no matter what its extent or purpose may be." (*Free Composition*, 129.) A coda that modulates away from the tonic may still prolong $\hat{1}$ on some high structural level, but on lower structural levels it creates tension and the anticipation of a return to the tonic.

54. Heinrich Schenker, *Das Meisterwerk in der Musik,* vol. 3 (Munich: Drei Masken Verlag, 1930), 29–54.

55. The harmonic tension is partially resolved by the arrival of E♭ minor at measure 589. The E♭-minor section that follows (mm. 589–95) is highly significant because it is part of a redevelopment and resolution of the E-minor theme first introduced so strikingly in the development at measures 284–99.

56. Twenty-three of the twenty-four fast (at least *allegro*) movements in the nine symphonies end with a tutti chord whose notes are all the same duration (although the oboe is omitted in the final chord of Symphony No. 1, III). Twenty-one of the twenty-four end fortissimo. Of course, the fact that the final chord is generally played tutti contributes to an extremely loud dynamic level.

Chapter 3: Secondary Parameters and Closure

1. Jan LaRue's *Guidelines for Style Analysis* (New York: W. W. Norton, 1970) provides a general description of secondary parameters. Other authors make specific contributions toward our understanding of secondary parameters. These include, among others: Wallace Berry, *Structural Functions in Music,* on texture; Robert Cogan and Pozzi Escot, *Sonic Design: The Nature of Sound and Music* (Englewood Cliffs, N.J.: Prentice-Hall, 1976), on register and timbre; Robert Cogan, *New Images of Musical Sound* (Cambridge, Mass.: Harvard University Press, 1984), on timbre; Robert Erickson, *Sound Structure in Music* (Berkeley: University of California Press, 1975), on timbre; Wayne Slawson, *Sound Color* (Berkeley: University of California Press, 1985), on timbre; David Epstein, *Beyond Orpheus* (Cambridge, Mass.: MIT Press, 1979), on tempo and durations; and Eugene Narmour, *Beyond Schenkerism,* on duration.

2. The studies of timbre are notable exceptions.

3. The lack of adequate terminology is evidence that music theorists and analysts have virtually ignored secondary parameters, and it is also at least partially a consequence of inadequacies in psychological theory.

4. This categorization in no way lessens the *importance* of rhythm. Other emergent properties of music, including tempo, are discussed below.

5. Such a definition of texture is suggested by LaRue in *Guidelines for Style Analysis,* 27.

6. Ulric Neisser, *Cognitive Psychology* (New York: Meredith Publishing, 1967), 10.

7. A perception is a psychological response to a physical stimulus. There is a close relationship between some perceptions of sounds and the physical characteristics of sound waves. The perception of pitch, for instance, is associated with the fundamental frequency of the sound wave. It is well known, however, that our perception of pitch is a complicated phenomenon that can be affected by changes in the intensity and form of a sound wave as well.

8. Those parameters having to do with tone color are exceptions. They are discussed below.

9. Therefore, it is inappropriate to label all secondary parameters "statistical," as Leonard Meyer does in "Toward a Theory of Style," 20. Statistics have to do with the tabulation and classification of numerical data, which we lack for some parameters.

10. There is a dissimilarity in our ability to identify simultaneous pitches and successions of pitches, as Diana Deutsch notes in her article "Music Recognition," *Psychological Review* 76 (1969): 300–307. As a result of experimentation, she concludes that we must have two neuronal systems: one for simultaneous pitches, and one for successions of pitches.

11. "Accent and grouping are the basic, if not neatly separable, modes of partitioning musical time and . . . meter is a secondary construct, imposed on the interaction of group structure and accent." William E. Benjamin, "A Theory of Musical Meter," *Music Perception* 1 (Summer 1984): 359.

12. An accented pulse may be defined as one that is "marked for consciousness" relative to others. See Cooper and Meyer, *The Rhythmic Structure of Music,* 4.

13. An exception is music that employs a continuum of pitch rather than specific and identifiable pitches. For instance, there are no discrete intervals in a melody consisting of several portamenti.

14. In discussing L. H. Shaffer's study of a concert pianist's performances of a different Bach fugue ("Analysing Piano Performance: a Study of Concert Pianists" in *Tutorials in Motor Behaviour,* ed. G. E. Stelmach and J. Requin [Amsterdam: North Holland, 1980]), John A. Sloboda reports: "A sequence repeated at increasingly higher pitch can signal the approach of a climax, and an appropriate response is often to increase the intensity for each repetition of the sequential pattern." See Sloboda, *The Musical Mind: The Cognitive Psychology of Music* (Oxford: Clarendon Press, 1985), 83.

15. See Max Meyer, "Experimental Studies in the Psychology of Music," *American Journal of Psychology* 14 (1903): 456–78. It is significant that the word we use to indicate the close of a musical passage—cadence—comes from the Latin word *cadere,* which means *to fall.*

16. The gaps in the pattern do not imply subsequent fills because from the standpoint of tonal pitch the descent through the tonic triad merely serves to prolong the tonic chord.

17. Of course, the system of tonality allows for the establishment of closure with an ascent to the tonic through the leading tone. For evidence that relaxation is associated with descending pitch patterns one might examine music not governed by the elaborate major/minor system of tonality, such as Gregorian chants. An overwhelming majority of final cadences in Gregorian chant end with descending motion. Over three-fourths of all Gregorian chants end with one of these descending, conjunct patterns: 2–1–2–1, 2–3–2–1, 3–1–2–1, or 1–3–2–1. The relatively rare final cadences that end with ascending motion almost always conclude with an ascending second. Frederic W. Homan, "Final and Internal Cadential Patterns in Gregorian Chant," *Journal of the American Musicological Society* 17 (1964): 66–77.

18. Robert Erickson, *The Structure of Music: A Listener's Guide* (Westport, Conn.: Greenwood Press, 1977), 28.

19. R. M. Ogden notes that this principle is "familiar to us in many expressions such as *zig-zag, tick-tock, knick-knack, flip-flop,* etc., all of which would sound strange if the syllables were reversed." R. M. Ogden, *Hearing* (New York: Harcourt, Brace & Co., 1924), 154. This of course does not generalize to all languages.

20. Therefore, it is not surprising that Heinrich Schenker believed only a descending, conjunct pitch pattern had the potential to be the *Urlinie* of a composition. It is possible to close a section or piece of music with an ascending pitch pattern, but such closure is necessarily dependent on forceful closure in processes defined by other parameters.

21. The fill is not always conjunct nor always complete. In nontonal music of the twentieth century that is characterized by especially wide leaps, a fill might be characterized by relatively small intervals such as thirds. Structural gaps are considered at length in Meyer, *Emotion and Meaning,* 145–57. See also Eugene Narmour, "The Melodic Structure of Tonal Music: A Theoretical Study" (Ph.D. diss., University of Chicago, 1974), chapter 4.

22. The pitch notation suggested by the Acoustical Society of America will be employed in this study; see preface. Leonard Meyer discusses melodic stretching at length in chapter 7 of his book *Style and Music: Theory, History, and Ideology* (Philadelphia: University of Pennsylvania Press, 1989).

23. The analytic graphs for the musical examples in this chapter do not distinguish between degrees of structural importance as determined by an analysis of several different parameters. Consideration is limited to the one parameter under discussion.

24. In part that is probably because notes in higher registers tend to be performed at higher dynamic levels, or at least are perceived to be at higher dynamic levels, than pitches in lower registers. The repetition of a pitch or pitch pattern at a higher pitch level will not be intensifying if it is heard as an echo, however. That is probably because the echo is considered a repetition or prolongation of the initial cognition, which is continued in the mind of the listener.

25. Our reactions to the tensity or restfulness of pitch patterns at different pitch levels are not solely a consequence of aural comparisons. That is, we seem to have an absolute sense that above a certain register any pattern will be somewhat tensive because it is high, even if it is low relative to other patterns, and below a certain register any pattern will be somewhat tensive because it is uncomfortably low. According to this view, then, we find a "middle" register most restful, and our concept of a "middle" register is probably based on the range of average human voices, from bass to soprano. In general, I believe, pitches at the top of the soprano range or above seem high, and pitches at the bottom of the bass range or below seem low. No doubt an individual's response to pitch levels is influenced by the range of his or her own voice as well.

26. Hermann Helmholtz, *On the Sensations of Tone as a Physiological Basis for the Theory of Music,* trans. and ed. Alexander J. Ellis, 2d ed. (New York: Dover Publications, 1954), 191–93. This is a translation of the 1877 edition of *Die Lehre von der Tonempfindungen als physiologische Grundlage für die Theorie der Musik* (Braunschweig: Verlag F. Vieweg & Sohn, 1863).

27. Consonant simultaneities do not require resolution, whereas dissonant ones do. For example, a very concordant sound such as a C-major triad can be consonant if used as the tonic in a piece or dissonant if employed as the dominant. For experimental evidence demonstrating how context determines judgments of consonance and dissonance, see A. D. Gardner and R. W. Pickford, "Relation Between Dissonance and Context," *Nature* 154 (1944): 274–75.

28. Further confusion resulted from the use of many different definitions of consonance, including pleasantness, fusion, and smoothness, among others.

29. The discussion that follows is based on the translation, *On the Sensations of Tone,* 159–233 and 330–50.

30. The number of beats per second is equal to the difference in the frequencies of the tones under consideration. For instance, the combination of two simple tones (that is, tones without upper partials) of 100 and 106 cycles per second will give six beats a second, which produce a discernible roughness. Fewer than six or more than 132 beats per second are not easily discernible and have little impact on our perception of roughness. Confirmation and refinement of Helmholtz's theories will be found in J. M. Geary, "Consonance and Dissonance of Pairs of Inharmonic Sounds," *Journal of the Acoustical Society of America* 67 (1980): 1785–89; Akio Kameoka and Mamoru Kuriyagawa, "Consonance Theory Part II: Consonance of Complex Tones and Its Calculation Method," *Journal of the Acoustical Society of America* 45 (1969): 1460–69; and Reinier Plomp and W. J. M. Levelt, "Tonal Consonance and Critical Bandwidth," *Journal of the Acoustical Society of America* 38 (1965): 548–60.

31. Thus, tones that have many or more intense upper partials are likely to be less concordant than tones with few or less intense upper partials. For experimental support of this theory, see C. F. Malmberg, "The Perception of Consonance and Dissonance," *Psychological Monograph* 25, no. 2 (1917–18): 93–133. Also, concordance varies with the mean frequency of the interval because at higher frequencies there are fewer audible partials and beats are too rapid to be distinct. Further, roughness tends to decrease with the magnitude of the interval, since for a large interval only the higher and weaker upper partials of the lower tone can produce beats with the partials of the higher tone.

32. In a study by van de Geer, Levelt, and Plomp, subjects judged the most dissonant (least consonant) intervals as the sharpest, most tense, and roughest. J. P. van de Geer, W. J. M. Levelt, and Reinier Plomp, "The Connotation of Musical Consonance," *Acta Psychologica* 20 (1962): 308–19.

33. Perhaps in order to increase the tension of the climactic V_7 in an authentic cadence, then, composers in the mid-to-late nineteenth century often substituted more discordant harmonies, such as V_7^9, V_7^{13}, $V_{5\flat}^7$, $V_{5\sharp}^7$, all of which maintain a dominant function. As a result of such substitution, there is a greater increase in concordance from the dominant chord to the following tonic chord, and closure is slightly enhanced. Another way of enhancing closure is to increase the concordance of the concluding tonic sonority rather than (or in addition to) increasing the discordance of the penultimate dominant. Mahler does that in the cadence that ends his Fifth Symphony, which concludes with octave Ds rather than a D-major triad.

34. It will be remembered that I am discussing *psychological* parameters, and hence loudness refers to our perception of loudness. It should not be confused with the physical attribute of loudness discussed in physics and acoustics.

35. One cannot rely upon the dynamic levels found in the score to indicate the loudness of a given passage. Various inherent factors can affect our perception of dynamics, including pitch, duration, instrumentation, spacing of sounds, masking effects, fatigue, and a tendency to focus on the highest or loudest tone when component frequencies are far apart.

36. This is especially true because of the low register, the short note values, and the staccato articulation. See Juan G. Roederer, *Introduction to the Physics and Psychophysics of Music* (New York: Springer-Verlag, 1973), 81–82.

37. One may not always be able to judge when the performers are playing as soft as possible, but it would seem that such judgments are far easier to make than those with respect to the loudest possible dynamic, since one can compare the soft dynamic level with a known limit: silence.

38. Such a decrescendo represents a kind of return—it leads back to the silence that preceded the first sound of the work. See Gisèle Brelet, "Music and Silence," in *Reflections on Art*, ed. Susanne K. Langer (Baltimore: Johns Hopkins University Press, 1958), 103–21.

39. So, for instance, the common fade-out of many popular tunes does not generally create satisfactory closure, although it will in the relatively rare event that the last thing you hear is a cadence.

40. This terminology is borrowed from Eugene Narmour, *Beyond Schenkerism*, 150.

41. See D. E. Berlyne, *Aesthetics and Psychobiology* (New York: Appleton-Century Crofts, 1971), 238; and P. G. Vos, "Pattern Perception in Metrical Tone Sequences," Psychological Laboratory, Report 73, University of Nijmegen, ON 06, 1–15. Experiments conducted by Herbert Woodrow indicate that louder notes tend to begin groupings and be perceived as slightly longer in duration than unstressed notes. See Herbert Woodrow, "A Quantitative Study of Rhythm," *Archives of Psychology* 14 (1909): 1–66.

42. Woodrow, "Quantitative Study of Rhythm," 1–66. Consider that the longer a note is held, the more it is separated from what follows.

43. Evidence for this is found not only in the music but also in treatises that discuss performance practice, including the *Micrologus* (c. 1026–28): "Towards the ends of phrases the notes should always be more widely spaced as they approach the breathing place, like a galloping horse, so that they arrive at the pause, as it were, weary and heavily." Claude V. Palisca, ed., *Hucbald, Guido, and John on Music: Three Medieval Treatises*, trans. Warren Babb (New Haven, Conn.: Yale University Press, 1978), 72.

44. Wendy L. Idson and Dominic W. Massaro, "Perceptual Processing and Experience of Auditory Duration," *Sensory Processes* 1 (1977): 317–37.

45. Alf Gabrielsson, "Interplay Between Analysis and Synthesis in Studies of Music Performance and Music Experience," *Music Perception* 3, no. 1 (Fall 1985): 74.

46. Within twelve measures the compound durations change from staccato quarter notes to eighth notes to eighth-note triplets, followed by sixteenth notes, thirty-second notes, and finally trilled notes.

47. See, for instance, the end of the first movement of Beethoven's String Quartet in C Major, op. 59, no. 3.

48. Of course other parametric processes and patterns in this excerpt might lead you to other groupings, but here we are only concerned with durational patterning.

49. Carl E. Seashore, *Psychology of Music* (New York: McGraw-Hill, 1938), 97.

50. Robert Cogan and Pozzi Escot have suggested that timbres can be organized according to their brightness, as determined primarily by where energy is concentrated in the spectrum and secondarily by the range of partials. The higher in the spectrum that energy is concentrated and the greater the range of partials, the brighter is the timbre. Although a "spectral scale" for groups and types of instruments is employed in their book, Cogan and Escot do not provide an explanation of how specific sounds might be perceived on a scale of brightness, and indeed such a system seems too complex to be practical. It remains unclear, too, whether listeners can differentiate brightness and darkness without being influenced significantly by register. See *Sonic Design,* 422–23.

51. See John M. Grey, "An Exploration of Musical Timbre" (Ph.D. diss., Stanford University, 1975); and David L. Wessel, "Low Dimensional Control of Musical Timbre," IRCAM Report Paris No. 12 (1978). The results are discussed in Jean-Claude Risset and David L. Wessel, "Explorations of Timbre by Analysis and Synthesis," in *The Psychology of Music,* ed. Diana Deutsch (Orlando, Fla.: Academic Press, 1982), 26–58. Other authors have proposed that timbre has more than two dimensions. Wayne Slawson, for example, specifies four dimensions of timbre in *Sound Color,* 57. Slawson discusses his theory in some detail and on pages 134–40 he reviews psychoacoustical studies of timbre.

52. We are more likely to perceive specific relationships between different sounds produced by the same instrument. For example, we tend to classify a person's voice according to whether it is brighter or darker, lighter or heavier, and so forth.

53. Quoted in Robert P. Morgan, "Stockhausen's Writings on Music," *Musical Quarterly* 61 (1975): 4.

54. So, for example, tone color has been defined as "The quality of sound, as distinct from its pitch; hence, the quality of sound that distinguishes one instrument from another." "Tone color," *The New Harvard Dictionary of Music.* Of course, timbre is much more complex than that. One cannot define a clarinet timbre or trumpet timbre, for instance, because the timbres of these (and other) instruments vary according to register and dynamics. We can, of course, learn the various timbres that an instrument can produce and consequently learn to recognize the sound of a particular instrument.

55. Seashore, *Psychology of Music,* 194–96.

56. Owing to the availability of electronically produced music, composers are now able to create timbres as well as control timbres in a way that was not possible until recently. It may be that "proper timbral control might lead to quite new architectures," as Risset and Wessel have suggested, but it remains to be seen whether any such architectures will be a result of timbral processes and patterns that lead to closure, or rather some other kind of timbral articulation. See Risset and Wessel, "Explorations of Timbre," 50.

57. For experimental evidence of such "implied polyphony" see Albert S. Bregman and Jeffrey Campbell, "Primary Auditory Stream Segregation, Perception of Order in Rapid Sequences of Tones," *Journal of Experimental Psychology* 89 (1971): 244–49.

58. Arnold Schoenberg, *Style and Idea,* ed. Leonard Stein with translations by Leo Black (London: Faber & Faber, 1975), 301.

Chapter 4: Secondary Parameters and Closure in Mahler

1. Deryck Cooke, *Gustav Mahler: An Introduction to His Music* (Cambridge: Cambridge University Press, 1980), 5.

2. Hans Tischler, "Mahler's Impact on the Crisis of Tonality," *Music Review* 12 (1951): 121.

3. The frequent and usually emphatic tonal closure found throughout the Eighth Symphony makes it exceptional. As Deryck Cooke has declared, "Apart from much clashing counterpoint in Part I, and

certain tonal disruptions in Part II, Mahler temporarily abandoned the more progressive elements of his style; instead he united his masterly middle-period orchestral polyphony with the firm tonality, monumental apparatus and all-embracing programmatic aim of the Second Symphony." Cooke, *Gustav Mahler,* 93.

4. Donald Mitchell, "Gustav Mahler," *The New Grove Dictionary of Music and Musicians* (1980), XI: 518.

5. Dika Newlin, *Bruckner, Mahler, Schoenberg,* 2d ed. (New York: W. W. Norton, 1978), 129.

6. Robert Bailey, *"Das Lied von der Erde:* Tonal Language and Formal Design." Paper read at the Forty-Fourth Annual Meeting of the American Musicological Society (October 21, 1978).

7. Christopher Orlo Lewis, *Tonal Coherence in Mahler's Ninth Symphony* (Ann Arbor, Mich.: UMI Research Press, 1984), 3–6. One need not agree with Lewis about the scope of Mahler's employment of the double-tonic complex in order to recognize and accept its importance in Mahler's music.

8. The order of the two inner movements of Symphony No. 6 remains controversial. Originally the *Andante moderato* was planned as the third movement, and the symphony was published that way by C. F. Kahnt. However, Mahler changed his mind about the order of movements while preparing the première of the symphony. At the première on May 27, 1906, the slow movement was played second and the Scherzo third. The symphony was subsequently republished with the revised order of movements. Some scholars believe that in his last years Mahler favored a return to the original order of movements. However, there is no documented evidence to support that view. For a more detailed discussion of the controversy, see Norman Del Mar, *Mahler's Sixth Symphony: A Study* (London: Eulenburg, 1980), 90–92.

9. The most extreme of these examples are *Nun seh' ich wohl, warum so dunkle Flammen* and the Scherzo of Symphony No. 6, neither of which contains a strong authentic cadence in the tonic. Very few are found in the other works mentioned above. For instance, *Um Mitternacht* has only one at the end (mm. 92–93), and in Symphony No. 3, I, there are only three authentic cadences in D minor, none of which are very strong (mm. 167–69 and its repeat 686–88, 208–9—though the tonic chord of resolution includes a major seventh—and 733–35). The latter movement ends in F major, not after an authentic cadence in F major but rather following a remarkable G♭ to G to F progression of major triads in measures 865–67.

10. There is no generally accepted label for this particular ♭II chord. (Of course, if the key were D major or D minor, the chord would be a German augmented sixth.) Throughout the book ♭II⁶# will be used to refer to a major triad that is built on the lowered second scale degree and contains an added augmented sixth.

11. See, for instance, measures 32, 35–36, and 41–42.

12. For examples see Symphony No. 1, II (mm. 22–23); No. 4, I (mm. 57–58); No. 4, III (mm. 16–17); No. 5, III (mm. 621–22); No. 6, I (mm. 56–57 and 443–44); No. 7, I (mm. 31–32 and 316–17); No. 8, II (mm. 242–43 and 779–80); No. 9, II (mm. 48–49 and 57–58); *Das klagende Lied,* II (mm. 154–58); and *Das Lied von der Erde,* I (mm. 392–93).

13. See, for instance, the discussion of the opening of Symphony No. 1 which accompanies Examples 4.4 and 4.6.

14. Michael Kennedy, *Mahler* (London: J. M. Dent & Sons, 1974), 80. Jim Samson maintains that "The important consequence of this contrapuntal independence is that the tensions and relaxation which propel the phrase are often achieved by means of dissonant/consonant relationships within a contrapuntal texture, rather than through tonal-harmonic progressions which possess independent ongoing properties." Jim Samson, *Music in Transition* (New York: W. W. Norton, 1977), 15.

15. The simple durational pattern in the cellos can be reduced to a series of quarter notes in the slowly increasing tempo.

16. Gustav Mahler, *Sämtliche Werke, Kritische Gesamtausgabe, herausgegeben von der Internationalen Gustav-Mahler-Gesellschaft, Wien,* 14 vols. and supplement (1963–88).

17. Where practical, the orchestration is indicated. On the other hand, where a single stave

contains a conflation of various individual parts, no instruments are designated.

18. Because of the slower tempo ("Etwas zurückhaltend") beginning at measure 159, the half-note compound duration that starts the measure is slightly longer than the preceding ones, and therefore it concludes an additive durational pattern.

19. At the end of the movement Mahler repeats the closing section of measures 135–62 at measure 416, this time transposed to the tonic and without the dynamic abatement to pianissimo. Abatements in components and registral pitch begin in measure 436 (as they did, correspondingly, in measure 155) and lead to component closure at measure 440, but instrumental parts are still marked fortissimo and there is a sense of urgency as a result of an accelerando beginning in measure 437 as well as an abbreviation of the original seven-and-one-half measure phrase (the end of measure 155 through measure 162) to a four-and-one-half measure phrase (the end of measure 436 through the end of measure 440). Thus, processes in durations and dynamics prevent any significant abating closure at measure 440. Instead, after some "false starts" Mahler concludes the movement with a fortissimo perfect authentic cadence played by the whole orchestra in measures 449–50.

20. Arnold Schoenberg, "Gedanke manuscript," *Journal of the Arnold Schoenberg Institute* 2 (October 1977): 24.

21. It should be noted that a dissolution can be intensifying or abating. The listener's perception of the function of a dissolution is determined primarily by processes in the parameters of dynamics and duration, and secondarily by processes in other parameters. A dissolution coupled with intensifications in dynamics and duration, for instance, would be strongly intensifying.

22. If the abatement ends before reaching significant closure, the listener may retrospectively assign closure to the abatement.

23. Natalie Bauer-Lechner, *Recollections of Gustav Mahler,* ed. and annot. Peter Franklin, trans. Dika Newlin (Cambridge: Cambridge University Press, 1980), 130.

24. Of course in Example 4.7 there is also an ascent to A5 and A6, which are heard as doublings of the A2 pedal.

25. By listing these three types I do not mean to imply that they are the only kinds of dissolutions found in Mahler's music, nor do I intend to suggest that there are always distinct differences among the three types. Both of these points should become clear in the discussion to follow.

26. The collapse is signaled by the harmonic shift in measure 66.

27. An abbreviated and varied repetition of section A in measures 146–88 is closed in a similar manner, though the dissolution in measures 176–81, which are conformant with measures 66–73, is followed by a second abating gesture in measures 181–88.

28. See also measures 98–103 and 402–7 in Symphony No. 2, III.

29. Measures 82–87 are conformant with measures 27–32, which mark the end of the first subsection of the scherzo. There is durational closure in measure 86, but because of the conformant relationship the listener expects the passage to conclude only after an ascent to A6 is achieved, as it was in measure 32. (Measures 62–91 are a varied and abbreviated restatement of mm. 1–32.) The anticipated A6 is not reached until measure 87.

30. Other examples of gestures of collapse are found in Symphony No. 2, III (mm. 98–103 and 402–7) and V (mm. 134–42); Symphony No. 4, I (mm. 121–25 and 164–66) and III (mm. 74–76, 89–91, and 210–12); Symphony No. 5, II (mm. 141–46) and III (mm. 129–31) and V (mm. 345–49); Symphony No. 6, II (mm. 94–99) and III (mm. 405–11); Symphony No. 7, II (mm. 28–30) and III (mm. 150–59); Symphony No. 8, I (mm. 173–77); Symphony No. 9, I (mm. 198–204); *Lied des Verfolgten im Turm* (mm. 9–10, 37–38, and 108–9); *Um Mitternacht* (mm. 17–20 and 65–68); and *Das Lied von der Erde,* VI (mm. 94–97 and 144–49). Donald Mitchell briefly mentions a few of these instances of collapse in his book *Gustav Mahler: Songs and Symphonies of Life and Death* (Berkeley: University of California Press, 1985), 124.

31. Following the dynamic climax in measure 144, the music rather quickly fades to a pianissimo high C7 pitch in the first violins at measure 147, after which generally falling pitch patterns throughout measures 147–56 lead to a single *ppp* cello line in measures 157–58 that recalls the opening two

measures of the movement. It is in measures 153–58 that one has the sense that the music dissipates, with repetitions of various melodic fragments and little sense of forward motion.

32. Leonard Bernstein, *The Unanswered Question: Six Talks at Harvard* (Cambridge, Mass.: Harvard University Press, 1976), 321.

33. See also measures 81–89 in Symphony No. 9, II, where the gesture of fragmentation ends the first large A section of the movement.

34. The closing phrase is first heard in measures 185–88 and later repeated with slight variations in measures 207–10, 232–36, 244–47, 424–26 (the end of a scherzo section!), and 441–44.

35. *Webster's New Twentieth Century Dictionary Unabridged,* 2d ed., s.v. "subside."

36. Instead, the A4 pitch in measure 93 is in some sense a resolution of the B♭/A discord at the end of measure 92 by octave transfer up.

37. The subsidence and textual closure at the end of the second movement allows Mahler to conclude with barely three measures of tonic harmony (mm. 508–10) after the dominant has been prolonged for 104 measures (mm. 404–507).

38. See, for instance, measures 369ff. and 544ff. in movements I and II, respectively, of Symphony No. 5.

39. Leonard G. Ratner, *Music, The Listener's Art,* 2d ed. (New York: McGraw-Hill, 1966), 315.

40. The effect is that of an augmented sixth chord over a pedal. The augmented sixth chord traditionally has a subdominant function, but here the chord has a dominant function. Consequently, its use exemplifies the attenuation of traditional tonal syntax. The avoidance of a traditional cadential progression here and elsewhere in the third movement indicates the declining influence of traditional tonal harmony in producing closure.

41. The passage under consideration is the only example of strong abating closure in the movement. Other examples of approach to the pedal tone through the triad are found in Symphony No. 1, IV (mm. 230–38); Symphony No. 6, IV (mm. 9–16); and *Das klagende Lied,* I (mm. 469–92).

42. The descent through E♭ is probably anticipated by the listener as a result of the repeated E♭ to D motion in measures 757–60: E♭ in the clarinet at measure 757 moves to D in the next measure, and the E♭ of measure 759 descends to D (in the horns and violin) at measure 760.

43. Mahler concludes the movement with a final closing gesture based on the fanfare motive (mm. 406–15). At first glance it seems that, because they are ascending, the fanfare patterns in the trumpet and flute at measures 406–11 do not support closure, but in the context of diminishing dynamics and longer durations they can be heard as fading echoes of the trumpet fanfare from measures 406–7. Two homogeneous durational and dynamic processes—one in the trumpet and flute fanfare music, and one in the bass drum—support closure, which is enhanced by the changes in compound timbre from a fairly rich compound timbre in measures 402–5, where the strings play *col legno* along with horns and low woodwinds, to the nearly pure flute timbre of measures 410–12. The final pizzicato Cs in the low strings articulate a specific point of conclusion and constitute a return to a more restful register, one that is an octave lower than the register at measure 401.

44. An examination of many more examples of this kind of subsidence would reveal the full extent of Mahler's inventiveness. Further examples of subsidence characterized by the repetition of a motive at successively lower registers are found in Symphony No. 4, I (mm. 36–37, 67–72, and 164–66); Symphony No. 5, I (mm. 27–34 and 145–52) and II (mm. 568–76); Symphony No. 6, I (mm. 50–56) and II (mm. 47–53); Symphony No. 7, II (mm. 76–82) and III (mm. 170–79 and 205–10); Symphony No. 9, II (mm. 569–78); and Symphony No. 10, I (mm. 34–35). Other instances of subsidence in which a more or less continually descending figure reaches closure on the note of the pedal or its octave can be found in Symphony No. 1, IV (mm. 230–38); Symphony No. 2, I (mm. 441–45) and III (mm. 577–81) and V (mm. 18–26 and 55–61); Symphony No. 3, I (mm. 110–30 and 209–24) and III (mm. 111–20); Symphony No. 5, I (mm. 23–27 and 53–60) and II (mm. 545–50) and III (mm. 618–21) and V (mm. 233–41); Symphony No. 6, III (mm. 110–11) and IV (mm. 9–16); Symphony No. 7, III (mm. 154–58); Symphony No. 8, I (mm. 41–46); *Das klagende Lied,* I (mm. 37–48, 230–43, and 469–

92); *Der Tamboursg'sell* (mm. 156–65); *Lob des hohen Verstandes* (mm. 7–10 and 126–29); and *Das Lied von der Erde,* VI (mm. 16–19 and 365–69).

45. There is, to be sure, a repeated G5–A5–F5 melodic cadential formula in the high woodwinds and first violins at measures 165, 167, and 168, but ongoing motion is created by the compound durational pattern of constant sixteenth notes in measures 163–72.

46. Other examples of reduction are found in Symphony No. 1, IV (mm. 149–66) and Symphony No. 2, I (mm. 226–43 and 418–26).

47. The reader will recall that, in an abatement, dynamic closure results when a passage fades to silence or to the softest possible dynamic level as judged by the listener.

48. The repetition of the same durational pattern in the violas in measures 384, 385, 386, 387, and the first part of 388 provides a basis of comparison for listeners to appreciate the slowing tempo.

49. The portamenti in the strings at measures 210–12 may give some listeners the impression of a collapse, but overall there is no sudden drop in pitch (note the prolonged high pitches in the flutes, for instance), and the dissolution continues for several measures.

50. There is dynamic closure as long as the listener believes that the music has faded to the softest possible dynamic level.

51. For other instances of subsidence characterized chiefly by diminishing dynamics and decreasing components, see Symphony No. 1, III (mm. 31–38 and 76–81) and IV (mm. 290–96 and 412–28); Symphony No. 2, I (mm. 109–17 and 247–53) and V (mm. 26–42 and 434–47); Symphony No. 3, I (mm. 156–63, 178–83, 414–23, 625–42, and 696–705) and II (mm. 18–19 and its repetitions) and IV (mm. 89–93) and V (mm. 116–20); Symphony No. 4, I (mm. 67–72 and 330–39) and II (mm. 195–200) and III (mm. 51–61 and 166–73); Symphony No. 5, II (mm. 500–519) and IV (19–22 and 84–86); Symphony No. 6, II (mm. 134–37) and IV (mm. 820–22); Symphony No. 7, III (mm. 51–52 and 65–66); Symphony No. 8, I (mm. 191–95); Symphony No. 9, I (mm. 239–43 and 448–54) and IV (mm. 144–47); *Das klagende Lied,* I (mm. 416–22 and 490–506); *Das irdische Leben* (mm. 128–36); *Nun will die Sonn' so hell aufgeh'n* (mm. 82–84); and *Das Lied von der Erde,* II (mm. 116–21) and VI (mm. 24–26, 155–58, 163–65, 320–33, and 425–29).

52. See the final measures of each song in the *Lieder eines fahrenden Gesellen* and *Kindertotenlieder,* as well as the ends of *Erinnerung, Frühlingsmorgen, Hans und Grethe, Nicht wiedersehen, Der Schildwache Nachtlied, Revelge, Ich bin der Welt abhanden gekommen,* and *Um Mitternacht.* Further examples are found in *Das klagende Lied,* I (mm. 169–75 and 416–22) and II (mm. 154–58); and *Das Lied von der Erde,* II (mm. 145–54) and III (mm. 115–18) and VI (mm. 50–54, 155–58, and 532–72); Symphony No. 1, IV (mm. 496–533); Symphony No. 2, II (mm. 276–95) and IV (mm. 31–35) and V (mm. 469–71 and 550–59); Symphony No. 3, I (mm. 114–25) and III (mm. 521–28 and 541–47) and IV (mm. 78–83) and VI (mm. 104–8); Symphony No. 4, I (mm. 97–101 and 234–38) and III (mm. 103–6); Symphony No. 5, III (mm. 305–9 and 417–18); Symphony No. 6, II (mm. 192–201) and IV (mm. 810–16 and 816–19); Symphony No. 7, I (mm. 296–98) and IV (mm. 257–59 and 390); Symphony No. 8, II (mm. 1404–20); and Symphony No. 9, II (mm. 364–68).

53. The longest E is held for three entire measures (511–13); consequently, closure occurs at the beginning of measure 517, the fourth measure of the extended D that follows.

54. See also Symphony No. 3, II, measures 18–19 and its repetitions. A similar gesture is found in Symphony No. 7, III, measures 51–52 and elsewhere, but there is only a suggestion of an authentic cadence because the penultimate chord has a minor third.

55. For a detailed discussion of the use of refrain lines in Mahler's vocal works, see Zoltan Roman, "Mahler's Songs and Their Influence on His Symphonic Thought" (Ph.D. diss., University of Toronto, 1970).

56. I agree with Norman Del Mar that measures 1–16 might best be considered a preface to the movement. See Del Mar, *Mahler's Sixth Symphony,* 52.

57. Here of course the motto is reduced to a sustained A-minor triad, rather than an A-major triad changing to A minor.

Chapter 5: Closing Observations

1. By *kinds* of parameters I mean durations, dynamics, pitch, timbre, and components.

2. The slow first movement of No. 10 does not conclude this way, although the slow final section of the Finale does. Neither movement of the Eighth Symphony can be considered slow, and neither ends with durational and dynamic closure.

3. See the conclusions of Symphony No. 1, III; No. 2, IV; No. 3, IV; No. 4, III (Example 4.31) and IV (Example 4.26); No. 5, IV; No. 6, II; No. 7, II and IV; and No. 9, IV (Example 4.12).

4. Concordant closure in measure 763 of Example 4.21 contributes to the strong repose.

5. See, for instance, Examples 3.12, 4.16, 4.22, 4.28, and 4.30.

6. For instance, see the discussions of Examples 4.6–4.7 (I: mm. 1–40 and 55–62), 4.16 (II: mm. 100–108), and 4.33 (IV: mm. 502–34).

7. See Examples 4.23–4.24 (II: mm. 76–85 and 196–209) and 3.12 (III: mm. 473–82); see also measures 55–61 and 134–42 of the fifth movement.

8. Closure in the episodic first part of the Finale, on the other hand, is generally created by several corresponding secondary parameters.

9. See, for example, measures 9–23, 115–27, and 156–63 in the first movement, and measures 137–43 in the fourth movement.

10. The first movement is notable for its length (875 measures) and the absence of weighty tonal harmonic closure. Indeed, outside of the march in measures 247–314 and its repetition later in the movement, simultaneous tonal pitch and harmonic closure is virtually nonexistent.

11. See measures 79–91, 182–97 (Example 4.30), and 238–44.

12. See measures 51–61, 89–106, 166–73, 210–22, 307–14, and 344–53 (Example 4.31) in the third movement, and measures 36–39, 72–75, 106–14, 119–122, and 174–84 (Example 4.26) in the last movement.

13. For instance, see measures 27–34, 53–60, 83–87, 145–52, 369–401 (Example 4.22), and 406–15 in the first movement, and measures 66–73 (Example 4.9), 175–88, 500–520, and 568–76 in the second movement.

14. See, for instance, measures 87–91 (Example 4.11), 162–72 (Example 4.25), 261–69, 401–9, and 435–46 (Example 4.17).

15. Deryck Cooke, *Gustav Mahler,* 90.

16. See measures 28–30, 44–48, 76–82, 118–21, 155–61, 205–10, 256–61, 288–93, and 337–43.

17. As, for example, in measures 154–58, 206–10, and 253–57.

18. For instance, see measures 31, 108, 217, 327, 366, and 432 of the first movement.

19. For example, brief durational closure is created on the downbeat of measure 180, but the abrupt reduction in texture to a *ff* unison in the horns calls attention to the unison as the beginning of another passage.

20. Many phrases in the adagio sections of the movement are articulated by an abrupt change in dynamics (usually a sudden reduction) often accompanied by a significant change in orchestration. See, for example, the articulations in measures 20, 24, and 28.

21. Michael Kennedy, *Mahler,* 128.

22. Symphony No. 3, IV, is an exception.

23. Other instances include Examples 4.2, 4.10, 4.16, 4.18, 4.21, 4.31, and 4.37.

24. See, for instance, measures 179–80 in the third movement of Symphony No. 9 and the articulation of phrases in measures 16–28 of Symphony No. 10, I.

25. See, for example, measures 145–46 in II and 173–74 in III of Symphony No. 5; measures 76–77 in I of Symphony No. 6; and measures 78–79 in both I and V of Symphony No. 7.

26. See, for instance, Examples 3.1, 3.12, 4.2, 4.8, 4.9, 4.11, 4.14, 4.17, 4.21, 4.22, 4.25, 4.28, 4.31, and 4.37.

27. Michael Kennedy, *Gustav Mahler,* 80.

28. This is Ratner's "pattern of dynamic curve." Leonard Ratner, *Music, The Listener's Art,* 315.

29. Ibid., 316.

WORKS CITED

The American Heritage Dictionary of the English Language. Edited by William Morris. Entry: "parameter." Boston: Houghton Mifflin, 1970.

Backus, John. *The Acoustical Foundations of Music.* New York: W. W. Norton, 1969.

Bailey, Robert. "*Das Lied von der Erde:* Tonal Language and Formal Design." Paper read at the Forty-Fourth Annual Meeting of the American Musicological Society, October 21, 1978.

Bauer-Lechner, Natalie. *Recollections of Gustav Mahler.* Edited and annotated by Peter Franklin, translated by Dika Newlin. Cambridge: Cambridge University Press, 1980.

Benjamin, William E. "A Theory of Musical Meter." *Music Perception* 1 (Summer 1984): 355–413.

Berlyne, D. E. *Aesthetics and Psychobiology.* New York: Appleton-Century Crofts, 1971.

Bernstein, Leonard. *The Unanswered Question: Six Talks at Harvard.* Cambridge, Mass.: Harvard University Press, 1976.

Berry, Wallace. *Structural Functions in Music.* Englewood Cliffs, N.J.: Prentice-Hall, 1970.

Bregman, Albert S. and Jeffrey Campbell. "Primary Auditory Stream Segregation, Perception of Order in Rapid Sequences of Tones." *Journal of Experimental Psychology* 89 (1971): 244–49.

Brelet, Gisèle. "Music and Silence." In *Reflections on Art,* edited by Susanne K. Langer. Baltimore: Johns Hopkins University Press, 1958.

Cogan, Robert. *New Images of Musical Sound.* Cambridge, Mass.: Harvard University Press, 1984.

Cogan, Robert and Pozzi Escot. *Sonic Design: The Nature of Sound and Music.* Englewood Cliffs, N.J.: Prentice-Hall, 1976.

Cone, Edward T. *The Composer's Voice.* Berkeley: University of California Press, 1974.

Cooke, Deryck. *Gustav Mahler: An Introduction to His Music.* Cambridge: Cambridge University Press, 1980.

Cooper, Grosvenor W. and Leonard B. Meyer. *The Rhythmic Structure of Music.* Chicago: University of Chicago Press, 1960.

Culicover, Peter W. *Syntax.* New York: Academic Press, 1976.

Del Mar, Norman. *Mahler's Sixth Symphony: A Study.* London: Eulenburg, 1980.

Deutsch, Diana. "Music Recognition." *Psychological Review* 76 (1969): 300–307.

Eliot, T. S. "The Hollow Men." In *Collected Poems, 1909–62.* New York: Harcourt, Brace & World, 1963.

Epstein, David. *Beyond Orpheus.* Cambridge, Mass.: MIT Press, 1979.

Erickson, Robert. *Sound Structure in Music.* Berkeley: University of California Press, 1975.

———. *The Structure of Music: A Listener's Guide.* Westport, Conn.: Greenwood Press, 1977.

Gabrielsson, Alf. "Interplay Between Analysis and Synthesis in Studies of Music Performance and Music Experience." *Music Perception* 3, No. 1 (Fall 1985): 59–86.

Gardner, A. D. and R. W. Pickford. "Relation Between Dissonance and Context." *Nature* 154 (1944): 274–75.

Geary, J. M. "Consonance and Dissonance of Pairs of Inharmonic Sounds." *Journal of the Acoustical Society of America* 67 (1980): 1785–89.

Grey, John M. "An Exploration of Musical Timbre." Ph.D. dissertation, Stanford University, 1975.

Hare, F. G. "Artistic Training and Response to Visual and Auditory Patterns Varying in Uncertainty." In *Studies in the New Experimental Aesthetics,* edited by D. E. Berlyne. New York: Halsted, 1974.

Helmholtz, Hermann. *Die Lehre von der Tonempfindungen als physiologische Grundlage für die Theorie der Musik.* Braunschweig: Verlag F. Vieweg & Sohn, 1863.

———. *On the Sensations of Tone as a Physiological Basis for the Theory of Music.* Translated and edited by Alexander J. Ellis, 2d ed. New York: Dover Publications, 1954. (Translation of 1877 edition of *Die Lehre von der Tonempfindungen.*)

Homan, Frederic W. "Final and Internal Cadential Patterns in Gregorian Chant." *Journal of the American Musicological Society* 17 (1964): 66–77.

Hopkins, Robert George. "Secondary Parameters and Closure in the Symphonies of Gustav Mahler." Ph.D. dissertation, University of Pennsylvania, 1983.

Idson, Wendy L. and Dominic W. Massaro. "Perceptual Processing and Experience of Auditory Duration." *Sensory Processes* 1 (1977): 317–37.

Kameoka, Akio and Mamoru Kuriyagawa. "Consonance Theory Part II: Consonance of Complex Tones and Its Calculation Method." *Journal of the Acoustical Society of America* 45 (1969): 1460–69.

Kennedy, Michael. *Mahler.* London: J. M. Dent & Sons, 1974.

Koffka, Kurt. *Principles of Gestalt Psychology.* New York: Harcourt, Brace & Co., 1935.

Kreitler, Hans and Shulamith Kreitler. *Psychology of the Arts*. Durham, N.C.: Duke University Press, 1972.

LaRue, Jan. *Guidelines for Style Analysis*. New York: W. W. Norton, 1970.

Lerdahl, Fred and Ray Jackendoff. *A Generative Theory of Tonal Music*. Cambridge, Mass.: MIT Press, 1983.

Lewis, Christopher Orlo. *Tonal Coherence in Mahler's Ninth Symphony*. Ann Arbor, Mich.: UMI Research Press, 1984.

Mahler, Gustav. *Sämtliche Werke, Kritische Gesamtausgabe, herausgegeben von der Internationalen Gustav-Mahler-Gesellschaft, Wien*, 14 vols. and supplement (1963–88).

Malmberg, C. F. "The Perception of Consonance and Dissonance." *Psychological Monograph* 25, No. 2 (1917–18): 93–133.

Meyer, Leonard B. *Emotion and Meaning in Music*. Chicago: University of Chicago Press, 1956.

————. *Explaining Music: Essays and Explorations*. Berkeley: University of California Press, 1973.

————. *Style and Music: Theory, History, and Ideology*. Philadelphia: University of Pennsylvania Press, 1989.

————. "Toward a Theory of Style." In *The Concept of Style*, edited by Berel Lang. Philadelphia: University of Pennsylvania Press, 1979.

Meyer, Max. "Experimental Studies in the Psychology of Music." *American Journal of Psychology* 14 (1903): 456–78.

Mitchell, Donald. "Gustav Mahler." *The New Grove Dictionary of Music and Musicians* (1980), XI: 505–31.

————. *Gustav Mahler: Songs and Symphonies of Life and Death*. Berkeley: University of California Press, 1985.

Morgan, Robert P. "Stockhausen's Writings on Music." *Musical Quarterly* 61 (1975): 1–16.

Narmour, Eugene. *Beyond Schenkerism: The Need for Alternatives in Music Analysis*. Chicago: University of Chicago Press, 1977.

————. "Some Major Theoretical Problems Concerning the Concept of Hierarchy in the Analysis of Tonal Music." *Music Perception* 1 (Winter 1983–84): 129–99.

————. "The Melodic Structure of Tonal Music: A Theoretical Study." Ph.D. dissertation, University of Chicago, 1974.

Neisser, Ulric. *Cognitive Psychology*. New York: Meredith Publishing, 1967.

New Harvard Dictionary of Music. Edited by Don Randel. Entries: "cadence" and "tone color." Cambridge, Mass.: Belknap Press, 1986.

Newlin, Dika. *Bruckner, Mahler, Schoenberg*, 2d ed. New York: W. W. Norton, 1978.

Odgen, R. M. *Hearing*. New York: Harcourt, Brace & Co., 1924.

Palisca, Claude V., ed. *Hucbald, Guido, and John on Music: Three Medieval Treatises*. Translated by Warren Babb. New Haven, Conn.: Yale University Press, 1978.

Piston, Walter and Marc DeVoto. *Harmony,* 5th ed. New York: W. W. Norton, 1987.

Plomp, Reinier and W. J. M. Levelt. "Tonal Consonance and Critical Bandwidth." *Journal of the Acoustical Society of America* 38 (1965): 548–60.

Ratner, Leonard G. *Music, The Listener's Art,* 2d ed. New York: McGraw-Hill, 1966.

Risset, Jean-Claude and David L. Wessel. "Explorations of Timbre by Analysis and Synthesis." In *The Psychology of Music,* edited by Diana Deutsch. Orlando, Fla.: Academic Press, 1982.

Roederer, Juan G. *Introduction to the Physics and Psychophysics of Music.* New York: Springer-Verlag, 1973.

Roman, Zoltan. "Mahler's Songs and Their Influence on His Symphonic Thought." Ph.D. dissertation, University of Toronto, 1970.

Samson, Jim. *Music in Transition.* New York: W. W. Norton, 1977.

Schenker, Heinrich. *Das Meisterwerk in der Musik,* Vol. 3. Munich: Drei Masken Verlag, 1930.

———. *Free Composition [Der freie Satz].* Edited and translated by Ernst Oster. New York: Longman, 1979.

Schoenberg, Arnold. "Gedanke manuscript." *Journal of the Arnold Schoenberg Institute* 2 (October 1977): 4–25.

———. *Style and Idea,* ed. Leonard Stein with translations by Leo Black. London: Faber & Faber, 1975.

Seashore, Carl E. *Psychology of Music.* New York: McGraw-Hill, 1938.

Slawson, Wayne. *Sound Color.* Berkeley: University of California Press, 1985.

Sloboda, John A. *The Musical Mind: The Cognitive Psychology of Music.* Oxford: Clarendon Press, 1985.

Smith, Barbara Herrnstein. *Poetic Closure: A Study of How Poems End.* Chicago: University of Chicago Press, 1968.

Tischler, Hans. "Mahler's Impact on the Crisis of Tonality." *Music Review* 12 (1951): 113–21.

Van de Geer, J. P., W. J. M. Levelt, and Reinier Plomp. "The Connotation of Musical Consonance." *Acta Psychologica* 20 (1962): 308–19.

Vos, P. G. "Pattern Perception in Metrical Tone Sequences." Psychological Laboratory, Report 73, University of Nijmegen, ON 06.

Webster's New Twentieth Century Dictionary of the English Language, 2d ed. Edited by Jean L. McKechnie et al. Entries: "interval" and "subside."

Wessel, David L. "Low Dimensional Control of Musical Timbre." IRCAM Report Paris No. 12, 1978.

Woodrow, Herbert. "A Quantitative Study of Rhythm." *Archives of Psychology* 14 (1909): 1–66.

APPENDIX: LIST OF REHEARSAL NUMBERS AND MEASURE NUMBERS IN MAHLER'S SYMPHONIES

Rehearsal Number	Symphony No. 1				Symphony No. 2					Symphony No. 3					
	I	II	III	IV	I	II	III	IV	V	I	II	III	IV	V	VI
1	18	1	1	1	25	1		15	10	14	20	24	18	7	9
2	36	15	9	13	43	21		27	26	27	34	34	32	22	21
3	44	23	19	19	48	39		36	43	38	50	53	41	35	33
4	59	32	27	30	64	64		44	59	49	70	69	49	45	41
5	71	44	39	37	74	86		55	70	65	79	95	57	52	51
6	84	52	45	55	97	133	60		78	77	93	121	71	65	59
7	100	60	50	67	117	150			97	91	109	136	85	78	71
8	117	68	61	86	129	164			115	99	128	152	101	86	79
9	131	82	71	102	143	175			131	110	144	176	115	96	92
10	143	97	83	120	164	183			142	118	158	192	123	107	100
11	151	108	96	136	179	196			162	132	170	203	132		108
12	163	118	102	143	196	210			173	148	192	229	137		116
13	180	133	113	153	208	235			183	164	202	244			124
14	189	143	122	157	226	261			194	171	217	256			132
15	207	159	132	167	244	285			210	185	233	285			143
16	225	171	138	175	254				238	194	243	310			149
17	243	191	145	189	278				263	209	251	347			157
18	257	199	149	205	291				275	225	260	362			168
19	271	212	158	222	300				297	239	269	374			174
20	279	219		231	325				310	247		382			182
21	298	229		238	336				325	256		402			198
22	312	237		254	353				343	266		414			206
23	323	251		274	372				349	273		432			224
24	333	259		282	392				363	289		441			234
25	344	270		290	404				380	302		454			245
26	358	285		297	420				395	315		464			252
27	364	303		312	441				418	331		485			268
28	372	312		317			1		434	351		498			276
29	385	322		327			31		448	369		510			284
30	400	332		337			57		455	380		529			296
31	416	340		346			85		472	398		541			308
32	424	348		353			103		484	410		557			316
33	436			371			120		493	424		575			
34				375			149		502	440					
35				388			177		512	455					

Rehearsal Number	Symphony No. 1 IV	Symphony No. 2 III	V	Symphony No. 3 I
36	404	190	526	463
37	422	212	536	472
38	428	235	550	482
39	436	257	560	492
40	448	272	582	506
41	458	288	602	514
42	480	308	618	522
43	490	328	629	530
44	496	348	640	539
45	533	368	656	546
46	555	384	672	554
47	574	407	696	564
48	581	417	712	574
49	588	441	726	583
50	597	457	740	595
51	608	481	752	605
52	623	500		615
53	632	521		625
54	639	545		632
55	649	560		643
56	657			658
57	671			671
58	679			684
59	696			691
60	712			700
61	723			719
62				737
63				754
64				762
65				772
66				778
67				787
68				793
69				804
70				816
71				824
72				832
73				846
74				857
75				863
76				871

Rehearsal Number	Symphony No. 4				Symphony No. 5				
	I	II	III	IV	I	II	III	IV	V
1	18	34	25	12	21	16	16	19	39
2	32	46	62	25	35	31	40	39	56
3	38	69	81	40	61	43	73	72	88
4	58	94	107	48	89	54	96	85	108
5	67	115	137	57	121	74	121		136
6	77	145	179	66	133	101	136		159
7	91	157	192	76	155	117	174		177
8	102	185	205	87	173	129	201		223
9	116	203	222	99	195	141	252		241
10	125	221	263	106	211	161	270		273
11	142	254	283	115	239	177	308		297
12	155	281	315	122	263	214	352		318
13	167	314	326	142	279	230	389		333
14	177	342		153	295	254	419		349
15	192			165	323	266	448		365
16	209				337	284	476		389
17	221				357	308	490		423
18	239				369	322	516		441
19	251				393	336	527		465
20	262					352	550		483
21	283					372	563		497
22	293					388	579		511
23	315					400	602		526
24	330					420	628		538
25						436	648		558
26						448	662		575
27						464	686		592
28						478	705		623
29						501	726		641
30						520	756		659
31						529	783		687
32						539	803		711
33						557			725
34									749
35									775

Rehearsal Number	Symphony No. 6		Symphony No. 7		Symphony No. 8 I	II	Symphony No. 9		Symphony No. 10 I
1	6	I	7	I	8	7	7	I	16
2	14		12		13	14	18		24
3	25		17		21	22	36		32
4	31		32		27	29	57		40
5	43		39		31	35	69		49
6	53		50		37	44	96		58
7	61		58		46	49	125		69
8	77		64		52	57	152		73
9	85		70		56	62	174		81
10	91		76		62	67	182		88
11	98		88		73	73	202		96
12	107		96		80	80	221		102
13	115		105		89	86	243		112
14	123		109		98	95	293		116
15	135		122		108	101	316		122
16	144		129		114	108	356		126
17	152		138		122	115	40	II	130
18	166		142		131	123	58		135
19	178		154		141	132	123		141
20	187		160		147	139	159		151
21	196		168		156	147	187		162
22	217		180		162	154	283		172
23	225		188		169	163	384		176
24	234		196		178	167	445		178
25	251		204		183	174	466		184
26	267		212		192	180	542		194
27	278		220		199	185	566		199
28	286		224		205	190	15	III	208
29	290		234		211	195	44		213
30	304		242		218	202	66		217
31	310		249		223	209	121		225
32	322		257		227	214	143		230
33	334		262		231	227	209		238
34	344		274		241	233	227		244
35	352		284		245	239	296		253
36	365		289		252	247	329		259
37	382		298		258	255	380		266
38	390		304		262	261	404		
39	402		313		268	266	446		
40	417		322		275	273	494		
41	429		328		282	279	554		
42	444		335		290	285	576		
43	457		343		296	293	592		

Rehearsal Number	Symphony No. 6		Symphony No. 7		Symphony No. 8 I	II
44	467		352		304	300
45	475		362		308	307
46	10	II	369		312	316
47	21		379		320	322
48	28		388		327	329
49	36		393		333	336
50	42		400		337	342
51	56		409		343	348
52	72		417		349	356
53	84		423		355	362
54	93		433		360	370
55	100		441		366	379
56	115		450		372	385
57	124		456		379	393
58	137		467		385	402
59	146		471		389	411
60	160		478		394	418
61	173		489		400	426
62	185		499		404	434
63	10	III	505		408	440
64	16		510		413	449
65	27		519		416	462
66	34		531		421	470
67	42		535		424	478
68	51		545		428	483
69	62		10	II	432	489
70	73		16		437	496
71	80		20		441	504
72	87		30		451	512
73	98		37		457	520
74	111		46		465	528
75	121		54		470	540
76	127		62		474	548
77	136		70		480	556
78	145		78		484	563
79	157		86		488	570
80	173		94		494	576
81	183		100		499	580
82	199		110		504	588
83	211		118		508	597
84	222		126		519	604
85	238		137		525	612

Rehearsal Number	Symphony No. 6		Symphony No. 7		Symphony No. 8 I	II
86	253		144		532	619
87	261		149		538	625
88	273		156		543	631
89	281		165		548	639
90	288		173		557	650
91	301		179		564	658
92	313		189		573	666
93	325		199			672
94	336		205			679
95	346		211			688
96	355		222			695
97	372		230			704
98	385		238			713
99	394		245			721
100	401		252			728
101	409		262			734
102	420		270			742
103	433		278			750
104	16	IV	286			758
105	39		295			768
106	49		302			780
107	65		312			788
108	82		318			797
109	98		326			804
110	114		334			812
111	122		337			818
112	132		7	III		825
113	139		15			833
114	149		24			841
115	160		30			849
116	176		38			858
117	191		46			868
118	205		54			876
119	217		62			884
120	229		72			894
121	239		78			906
122	258		86			916
123	271		95			927
124	288		100			937
125	296		108			946
126	304		116			956
127	313		127			964
128	328		135			970

Rehearsal Number	Symphony No. 6	Symphony No. 7	Symphony No. 8 II
129	336	140	978
130	352	150	986
131	364	160	993
132	372	164	1001
133	381	175	1005
134	397	179	1013
135	415	188	1017
136	426	197	1023
137	441	206	1027
138	449	215	1031
139	458	223	1036
140	479	231	1042
141	489	241	1047
142	504	244	1055
143	520	255	1063
144	537	261	1070
145	550	271	1079
146	561	277	1083
147	575	287	1087
148	586	293	1095
149	598	303	1102
150	610	311	1110
151	626	319	1117
152	634	326	1126
153	642	334	1134
154	650	343	1138
155	660	351	1142
156	668	359	1149
157	678	367	1158
158	686	375	1164
159	700	381	1172
160	712	391	1180
161	728	398	1186
162	744	407	1195
163	765	415	1199
164	773	423	1205
165	790	428	1213
166	808	439	1219
167		446	1223
168		454	1228
169		464	1232
170		471	1238

Rehearsal Number	Symphony No. 7	Symphony No. 8 II	Rehearsal Number	Symphony No. 7	Symphony No. 8 II
171	479	1243	211	295	1494
172	487	1249	212	303	1500
173	493	1257	213	311	1506
174	498	1265	214	319	1512
175	8 IV	1273	215	327	1516
176	15	1277	216	335	1520
177	23	1285	217	341	1524
178	31	1291	218	351	1528
179	38	1299	219	359	1538
180	46	1305	220	367	1552
181	54	1310	221	375	
182	64	1316	222	382	
183	71	1320	223	1 V	
184	79	1324	224	11	
185	85	1329	225	17	
186	93	1336	226	25	
187	99	1344	227	33	
188	111	1352	228	43	
189	122	1356	229	49	
190	126	1360	230	56	
191	134	1364	231	64	
192	142	1368	232	70	
193	149	1372	233	79	
194	158	1380	234	89	
195	166	1388	235	98	
196	176	1394	236	105	
197	187	1404	237	113	
198	194	1413	238	120	
199	199	1421	239	128	
200	207	1429	240	136	
201	215	1437	241	143	
202	222	1445	242	153	
203	232	1454	243	161	
204	240	1459	244	168	
205	247	1464	245	176	
206	255	1468	246	184	
207	262	1472	247	193	
208	271	1478	248	200	
209	279	1482	249	209	
210	288	1486	250	217	

Rehearsal Number	Symphony No. 7	Rehearsal Number	Symphony No. 7
251	224	286	504
252	231	287	512
253	241	288	521
254	249	289	529
255	256	290	537
256	264	291	546
257	273	292	553
258	281	293	558
259	289	294	566
260	297	295	573
261	305	296	581
262	311	297	585
263	320		
264	328		
265	337		
266	345		
267	353		
268	360		
269	368		
270	377		
271	385		
272	392		
273	400		
274	409		
275	415		
276	425		
277	433		
278	441		
279	449		
280	457		
281	465		
282	473		
283	479		
284	488		
285	496		

INDEX OF MUSICAL EXAMPLES

INDEX